Transitional Economic Policy
and Policy Options
in Tanzania

Edited by
Professor Samuel M. Wangwe
Dr. Haji H. Semboja
and Dr. Paula Tibandebage

MKUKI NA NYOTA PUBLISHERS
DAR ES SALAAM

Published for the Economic and Social Research Foundation by
Mkuki na Nyota Publishers
6 Muhonda Street, Mission Quarter, Kariakoo
P.O. Box 4246, Dar es Salaam
Tanzania

© Economic and Social Research Foundation (1998)

ISBN 9976 973 41 1

Distributed outside Africa by
African Books Collective Ltd
27 Park End Street
Oxford OX1 1HU
UK

Printed and bound by Wolsey Hall Print Services
7 Thamesview Industrial Park, Abingdon, Oxfordshire, UK

Table of contents

List of abbreviations

ARI	-	Acute Respiratory Infections
ATC	-	Air Tanzania Corporation
BIS	-	Basic Industry Strategy
BOT	-	Bank of Tanzania
CAB	-	Civil Aviation Board
CAMARTEC	-	Centre for Agricultural Mechanisation and Rural Technology
CEDAW	-	Convention on the Elimination of All Forms of Discrimination Against Women
CPCT	-	Cleaner Production Centre of Tanzania
CRC	-	Convention on the Rights of the Child
CRDB	-	Cooperative Rural Development Bank
CSRP	-	Civil Service Reform Programme
CTI	-	Confederation of Tanzania Industries
DANIDA	-	Danish International Development Agency
DCA	-	Directorate of Civil Aviation
DEL	-	Direct Exchange Line
DIA	-	Dar es Salaam International Airport
EAC	-	East African Community
ERP	-	Economic Recovery Programme
ESAP	-	Economic and Social Action Programme
FIR	-	Flight Information Region
GCB	-	Grassroots Capacity Building
GDP	-	Gross Domestic Product
GTZ	-	German Bilateral Aid Agency
HPTC	-	High Precision Technology Centre
HRDS	-	Human Resource and Development Survey
IDA	-	International Development Agency
ILO	-	International Labour Organization
IFEM	-	Interbank Foreign Exchange Market
IFI	-	International Financial Institution
IMF	-	International Monetary Fund
IPC	-	Investment Promotion Centre
IPI	-	Institute for Production Innovation
IRP	-	Integrated Roads Projects
KIA	-	Kilimanjaro International Airport
KREP	-	Kenya's Rural Enterprises Programme
LFS	-	Labour Force Survey
MODWAC	-	Ministry of Community Development, Women's Affairs and Children
MOF	-	Ministry of Finance
MPC	-	Monetary Policy Committee
MSPF	-	Mineral Sector Policy Strategy Framework
MTNRE	-	Ministry of Tourism, Natural Resources and Environment
MVA	-	Manufacturing Value Added
MWCT	-	Ministry of Works, Communication and Transport
NASACO	-	National Shipping Agencies Corporation
NBC	-	National Bank of Commerce
NBFI	-	Non Bank Financial Institution
NEAP	-	National Environmental Action Plan

NESP	-	National Economic Survival Programme
NGOs	-	Non Governmental Organizations
NIEs	-	Newly Industialized Economies
NMC	-	National Milling Corporation
NPA	-	National Programme of Action
NUWA	-	National Urban Water Authority
OGL	-	Overseas General Licence
O&E	-	Organization and Efficiency
PEs	-	Public Enterprises
PMO	-	Prime Minister's Office
PRIDE	-	Programme for Rural Integration and Development
PSRC	-	Parastatal Sector Reform Commission
R&D	-	Research and Development
RETCOs	-	Regional Transport Companies
RPFB	-	Rolling Plan and Forward Budget
S&T	-	Science and Technology
SAC	-	Structural Adjustment Credit
SADC	-	Southern Africa Development Community
SAP	-	Structural Adjustment Programme
SDA	-	Social Dimensions of Adjustment
SGR	-	Strategic Grain Reserve
SIDA	-	Swedish International Development Agency
SIDO	-	Small Scale Industries Development Organization
SMEs	-	Small and Medium Scale Enterprises
STAMICO	-	State Mining Corporation
TANESCO	-	Tanzania Electric Supply Company
TANEXA	-	Tanzania Exporters Association
TAZARA	-	Tanzania Zambia Railway Authority
T-bills	-	Treasury Bills
TBS	-	Tanzania Bureau of Standards
TCFB	-	Tanzania Central Freight Bureau
TEMDO	-	Tanzania Engineering and Manufacturing Design Organization
THA	-	Tanzania Harbours Authority
TIRDO	-	Tanzania Industrial Research and Development Organization
TISCO	-	Tanzania Industrial Studies and Consulting Organization
TPH	-	Tonnes Per Hectare
TPTC	-	Tanzania Posts and Telecommunications Corporation
TRA	-	Tanzania Revenue Authority
TRC	-	Tanzania Railway Corporation
TRIP	-	Trade Related Intellectual Property
Tshs	-	Tanzania Shillings
TTCL	-	Tanzania Telecommunications Corporation Ltd
UDA	-	Usafiri Dar es Salaam (Dar es Salaam Transport)
UK-ODA	-	United Kingdom Overseas Development Agency
UN	-	United Nations
UN-DESD	-	United Nations Department of Economic and Social Development
UNCTAD	-	United Nations Conference on Trade and Development
UNDP	-	United Nations Development Programme

Introduction

Tanzania's socio-economic development has been guided by the principles that were laid down in the 1960s soon after attaining independence. The Arusha Declaration charted out a development perspective based on the principles of socialism and self-reliance. This development pattern put emphasis on investments in the social sectors to meet basic needs, placed most investments in the public sector and envisaged the transformation of the productive sectors. However, as manifested by the outcome of these development efforts, certain signs of strain and imbalances began to appear towards the end of the 1970s.

By the end of the 1970s the steady progress that had been made in economic growth and in meeting the basic needs of the population had been put under stress due to problems in the productive sector. The capacity of the economy to support the delivery of basic social services came under so much strain that some of the achievements began to be reversed. These reversals had an adverse effect on the quantity and quality of basic social services. By the end of the 1970s, there was an imbalance between the level of national earnings and the level of consumption. These imbalances were manifested in the growing budget deficit, balance of payments, a widening gap between investment and domestic savings and the intensification of inflationary pressures. All these were indicators of a society living beyond its means.

The development experience of the 1970s suggests that the economic crisis that emerged in the 1980s was precipitated by both external and internal factors. The major external factors were associated with trends in world prices, the break-up of the East African Community (EAC) and the Kagera War. From the policy-making point of view, however, internal factors are more amenable to influence through domestic economic management. The most important aspect of the economic management problem arose from the adoption and use of inappropriate policies. For example distorted agricultural pricing policies, the creation of public monopolies, especially in the sphere of commerce, which stifled private initiative, and the top down approach to development administration did not promote genuine local participation in development, and excessive administrative controls of the economy often were pitched against market forces.

The economic crisis of the 1980s necessitated the introduction of economic reforms that brought about fundamental changes in the approach to the management of the economy. The single decade of implementing economic reforms has produced signs of economic recovery, but that experience has given rise to further challenges relating to the management of these reforms. The fact that economic reforms have been put in place is both an opportunity and a challenge for the new government (1995). The purpose of this book is to assess the experience obtained by having adopted economic reforms as one economic management approach, to draw lessons from that experience, to take stock of the challenges and outstanding issues, and to put forward some policy and economic management options for the third phase government (1995-2000). This book serves two purposes. First, it identifies development challenges which the third phase government is expected to grapple with. Second, it establishes a benchmark on the basis of which future evaluations could be made.

The book is organized as follows. Chapter 1 presents an overview of the recent performance of the economy and the progress made in the implementation of economic reforms up to the end of the second phase government. Chapter 2 examines developments in the fiscal, monetary and financial sectors. Chapter 3 addresses issues in the productive sectors, namely, agriculture, mining and industry. Economic services (transport and communications, energy and water) are explored in Chapter 4, while Chapter 5 addresses the social sectors (education and health). Cross-sectoral issues such as exports, science and technology, environment, the labour market and employment, civil service reform, parastatal sector reform, the role of the state, private sector development, and external resource inflow are discussed in Chapter 6. Chapter 7 is a summary of the findings and recommendations, and is followed by the conclusion.

1. Recent economic performance and progress in economic reforms

Current status

Economic policy reform initiatives in Tanzania date back to 1981 and cover four main programmes: the National Economic Survival Programme (NESP) (1981/82); the Structural Adjustment Programme (SAP) (1982/83-1984/85); the Economic Recovery Programme (ERP) (1986/87-1988/89); and the Economic and Social Action Programme (ESAP) (1989/90-1991/92). Since 1993/94, the three-year Rolling Plan and Forward Budget (RPFB) has replaced the Five-Year Plans of the 1960s and 1970s and has also replaced the shorter-term programmes of the 1980s. Since the RPFB was introduced in 1992, progress has been made towards articulating sectoral objectives, policies, strategies and priorities within the overall macro-economic policy framework.

The structural adjustment policies that were adopted contained at least two components. First, there was a concern to "get prices right" whereby prices of foreign exchange, capital and domestic goods and services would reflect relative scarcities. Second, the perceived over-extension of the state into production, distribution and marketing led to a programme to reduce the role of the state in the economy. Public sector reforms and financial liberalization are part of this programme. The main focus since the launching of structural adjustment programmes has been to pursue an active exchange rate management policy with the aim of achieving an equilibrium through a market-based exchange rate, which would defend the external competitiveness of the shilling.

Between 1986 and 1992 the exchange rate of the Tanzania shilling was discretionarily adjusted. This led to a cumulative depreciation of the real effective exchange rate of about 90 percent over the period, and the premium in the parallel market was substantially reduced from its peak of over 800 percent in 1985 to about 30 percent in early 1992. To complement these initiatives, the government steadily expanded the "own funds" import scheme originally introduced in 1984, under which import licences were provided freely to importers not requesting foreign exchange from the Bank of Tanzania (BOT). The use of the "own funds facility" has declined somewhat from the peak of US$460 million in 1986. This is due to the introduction of such measures as the establishment of the Overseas General Licence (OGL) scheme, the progressive narrowing of the OGL import negative list from 1988, and the introduction of the Bureau de Change System. Nevertheless, the "own funds" facility continues to account for one third of total imports.

Several export promotion schemes complemented the discretionary adjustments in the exchange rate. The export retention scheme originally introduced in 1982 was expanded in 1986 allowing 50 percent foreign exchange retention for non-traditional exports and 10 percent for traditional exports. Such measures were aimed at enhancing export competitiveness.

The major turnaround in the exchange regime occurred in April 1992, with the integration of the then large parallel market into a formal private foreign exchange market in the form of bureaux de change. This opened up one segment of the market to the forces of demand and supply. These changes followed the enactment of the Foreign Exchange Act, 1992, replacing the Exchange Control Ordinance, which was seen to be incompatible with the dynamic macro-economic policies adopted under the ERP. The objectives of the short run exchange rate policy, and of the creation of the bureaux were:

(a) to bring some of the illegal foreign exchange transactions into the open
(b) to provide greater flexibility in exchange rate management, and
(c) to provide timely and useful information on forex market conditions.

Towards the end of 1993, the foreign exchange market operations were fine-tuned by the Bank of Tanzania so that:

(a) bureaux were permitted to maintain accounts at more than one commercial bank and various limits were uplifted or removed altogether, and
(b) parastatals selling their retention funds were allowed to tender their funds to the bureaux.

In July 1993, the Bank of Tanzania started to conduct weekly forex auctions. The objective was to improve the efficiency with which the official foreign exchange (including balance of payment support) was being allocated, through market determined exchange rates and providing a mechanism for mopping up excess liquidity in the economy. The latter resulted largely from poor fiscal performance in the 1992/93 fiscal year, which was exacerbated by the monetary expansion impact of the Bank of Tanzania's raw gold purchase and the debt conversion schemes which injected an equivalent of around 20 percent of the money stock into the economy during one year.

During the period of July 1993 to June 1994, the Bank of Tanzania conducted a total of 48 auctions, and sold US$155.4 million, equivalent to Tanzania Shillings (Tshs) 75.4 billion, to the bureaux and commercial banks. The BOT set the official selling rate for the US dollar as the weighted average rate of successful bids in the weekly auction. The official buying rate was set at a margin of 2.5 percent below the selling rate. The success of the foreign auctions, which was considered as a milestone towards attainment of the convertibility of the shilling for current account transactions, and the resulting dealers' sophistication cleared the way for the introduction of the interbank foreign exchange market (IFEM) on June 20, 1994. This mechanism, which was set up to replace the auctions, had the following objectives:

(a) to allow banks and other authorized dealers to play an active role in developing financial markets and instruments to serve their customers better
(b) to increase the efficiency with which the limited foreign exchange resources in Tanzania are deployed
(c) to establish a more realistically determined exchange rate, and
(d) to create an enabling environment for foreign investment in the financial and other sectors of the economy.

The interbank foreign exchange market was organized as an open outcry system whereby a coordinator from the Bank of Tanzania invites authorized dealers to offer to buy or sell US dollars in various amounts and rates. Whenever a buyer and a seller agree, a trade deal is concluded.

During the first period in which the IFEM was in operation (June 1994 up to October 1995) a total of about US$440 million have been supplied to the market. Of this, US$422.4 million (96 percent) were actually bought by commercial banks and authorized dealers. Unlike the foreign exchange auctions, where the Bank of Tanzania was the sole supplier, the interbank foreign exchange market is supplied by other dealers as well, inparticular the National Bank of Commerce (NBC). Up to the end of October 1995, the NBC was the largest supplier of foreign exchange to the market, accounting for 52 percent of the total amount supplied. The Bank of Tanzania accounted for 30 percent, and the remaining 18 percent was supplied by other banks and authorized bureaux. On average, the monthly amount supplied in the market amounted to US$25.9 million, or about US$6.5 million per week. The foreign exchange sold by the BOT in the IFEM is largely from donor balance of payments support.

Economic growth has responded favourably to economic reform efforts with the rate of economic growth rising from an average of 2 percent between 1981 and 1985 to an average of about 4 percent during 1986 to 1994. While there has been an improvement in macro-economic stability and in growth performance, further improvements in these areas or even the sustainability of the current achievements has been threatened mainly by institutional and structural constraints. The most challenging of these constraints are manifested in the persistent budget and balance of payment deficits (with official exports meeting only one-third of the import bill), the low level of domestic savings and continuing inflationary pressures. The ongoing institutional reforms include financial sector reform, civil service reform, parastatal sector reform, and planning and budgetary reforms. These reforms are complicated both by the constituent interests they touch upon and by the limited administrative capacity of the state to implement reforms.

The macro-economic imbalances can be attributed primarily to major weaknesses in the fiscal performance that have persisted since 1992/93 (relieved by a temporary improvement in the second half of 1993/94), and to the rather slow pace of some critical structural reforms. Key contributing factors were the widespread customs exemptions and tax evasion that undermine revenue collections, and weak administration expenditure control. The slow pace of the civil service reforms and the related but much needed review of the civil service compensation policy are continuing to have a negative impact on the management of expenditure control. The objective of balancing the budget was expected to be realized through abiding by government expenditure ceilings and reducing the budget deficit. However, during the period of economic reforms the overall budget deficit has not been eliminated.

The growth of money supply has not been effectively controlled. Between June 1986 and June 1993, the overall annual credit growth averaged 30.5 percent. While net claims on the government increased at an average annual rate of 21.3 percent credit, those of other sectors grew at a much faster rate averaging 44.2 percent per annum.[1] The magnitude of credit available to the government varied with the external financial inflows, particularly counterpart revenues. Recourse to bank borrowing every time there is a shortfall in external financial support indicates that internal balance has not yet been achieved and that the budget deficit would have been worse had dependence on foreign financing not been as high as it was. Largely because of these failures inflation has remained high (at above 20 percent).

The trade deficit has not been eliminated. Exports can only finance about 30 to 40 percent of the import bill. The real depreciation of the exchange rate notwithstanding, imports have continued to grow. Nevertheless, the composition of imports has changed in favour of consumer goods on one hand and a shift from capital goods imports to transport equipment (mostly light commercial vehicles) on the other. It is doubtful whether there has been a switch in expenditures to activities that are capable of generating long-term sustainable growth, despite the structural adjustment measures.

The total foreign debt has increased from US$4.3 billion in 1986 to US$7.5 billion in 1993. As a share of the Gross Domestic Product (GDP), the debt increased from 103 percent in 1986 to 285 percent in 1992. The debt service ratio has remained low (12 to 16 percent of the exports), largely due to a rescheduling after the Paris Club regulations were met.

Measures to liberalize trade include removing quantitative restrictions, permitting holders who own funds to import goods that are not in the negative list, reducing tariffs and rationalizing the tariff system. Import liberalization threatened the survival of domestic industry even as it improved access to imported intermediate inputs and capital goods.

In agriculture, trade liberalization took the form of liberalizing the distribution of inputs and liberalizing agricultural marketing. Bottlenecks to internal trade (e.g., roadblocks restricting trade between different regions in Tanzania) were removed. The trend towards eliminating consumer subsidies on maize flour, reducing transport subsidies, eliminating fertilizer subsidy, and reducing the role of the National Milling Corporation (NMC) to that of a buyer of the last resort continued while the already important role of private traders was legalized. This effectively ended the monopoly position of the NMC. At the same time the monopoly of agricultural marketing boards was reduced considerably and marketing boards were restructured to suit the new competitive environment.

The private sector, however, has moved into agricultural marketing more gradually than was envisaged partly because of an inadequate legal and regulatory framework. Legislation enacted in 1993 and the accompanying regulations issued during 1994 finally cleared the way for private sector competition in the marketing and processing of the major traditional export crops, where the strengthening of such competition has been an important goal. A revision of the legislation and other regulations has enabled movement towards a free, fair, and competitive agricultural marketing and processing system for major crops. In some surplus producing areas, however, the poor state of the road networks, especially in the rural areas, has inhibited the movement of agricultural products to markets. This, coupled with the failure of private trade to move in fast and fill the gaps left by the retreating marketing boards, has been associated with agricultural marketing difficulties in some areas.

The overall rate of investment in Tanzania has been high (at about 20 percent) even during the crisis years of 1980 to 1985. The rate of investment increased to an average of 34.6 percent during 1986 to 1992.[2] The fact that the import content of investment is high may have exaggerated the increase in the investment rate after 1986 when the exchange rate was being actively adjusted. More importantly, this high investment rate could have been used more efficiently to produce a higher GDP growth rate than the average growth rate of four percent actually achieved over the 1985 to 1995 period. Furthermore, a most notable feature of the investment behaviour is the shift in favour of private sector investment. The share of private investment in the total investment increased from about 50 percent in the mid-1970s to 60 percent in 1986 and further to 70 percent in the early 1990s. This shift partly reflects the slow-down of investment in the parastatal sector and partly the private sector's response to economic liberalization and the improved attitude of the government towards the private sector. However, it is also notable that the structure of investment has shifted towards quick-yielding commercial investment, suggesting that the private sector still perceives uncertainty in the investment climate. There has been little success in attracting direct foreign investment. This illustrates the importance of policy predictability and certainty in the creation of a conducive climate for medium to long-term investments, which are crucial to sustained economic growth and development. In addition, in order to attract foreign private investment the necessary supporting infrastructure (telephone, energy, transportation, financial and legal framework, etc.) must be in place and the government must pursue stable and predictable macro-economic policies leading to low (single-digit) inflation rates, etc. A stable political system is, of course, an added strong advantage.

In recent years, Tanzania has made major progress towards putting in place a general policy environment that is more favourable to private sector expansion and growth. Most restrictive regulations and controls have been removed. The country is moving from its previous reliance on control mechanisms toward a predominantly market-oriented environment. There is an attempt to reduce government involvement in direct productive activities. A major challenge is that these changes are taking place in the context of an embryonic private sector and a state with reduced and weakened capacity to formulate and manage major economic reforms.

Challenges and outstanding issues

The rate at which the labour force is growing exceeds the rate at which new jobs are being created. This situation is leading to social tensions and could become a major source of social exclusion in Tanzania. Such a development could threaten to rend the social fabric. The need to create more job opportunities and generate more broad-based employment should be seen as a major challenge to the reduction of poverty and the fostering of social integration.

During the period of socio-economic crisis, the administrative and managerial capacity of the state deteriorated. While the capacity to plan and manage the economy was eroded, the demands put on the state to manage economic reforms and formulate development programmes that could lead to sustainable human development were greater than ever. A major obstacle to the effective coordination and implementation of the intended reforms was and still is the weak capacity of the state itself and its related institutions. It is for this reason that the coordinating role has often been directed from outside the country. The challenge to be faced is how to build a strong local capacity to manage the social, political and economic reforms both now and in the future.

The effect of growth performance on poverty alleviation is uncertain. Questions are being raised as to whether the achieved growth performance will also be accompanied by economic transformation. While living conditions have generally improved, there is no clear evidence that the incidence of poverty has declined with the reforms. The available evidence is debatable. However, there appears to be greater agreement that the very poor may have slipped into deeper poverty even though the overall level of poverty may have been reduced. About half the population still lives in poverty and the majority of the poor live in the rural areas. In the medium to long-term, the country needs a higher growth rate of 8 to 10 percent within the framework of a development strategy that integrates poverty alleviation concerns. Recently, the government has indicated its intentions to develop such a strategy. However, the actual design and formulation of such a development strategy has not been worked out.

The Social Dimensions of Adjustment (SDA) component on research and policy studies has been implemented and many studies on poverty have been produced. The results of some of these studies have been presented in several conferences and workshops. However, a major weakness in the strategy to alleviate poverty has been the failure to use the research results to formulate policies that integrate poverty concerns with development. This suggests that the link between research studies and the policy making process has not been established.

The transition to economic liberalization has also meant a weakened central policy direction at macro and sectoral level. A major weakness in the management of economic reforms has been the absence of a mechanism to develop a clear policy on the basis of which various components of economic reforms could be coordinated. Consequently, a series of institutional changes and economic reforms are being introduced without being directed by effective strategic long-term priorities.

Policy options

The economic record so far suggests that many economic reform elements are necessary and need to be retained or even pursued more vigorously. For instance, it has shown that macro-economic stability is necessary for rapid and sustained economic growth. In addition, it has revealed the importance of functioning competitive markets if resources are to be allocated effectively and prices to be determined rationally. However, there are still several gaps that must be reconsidered in the design and implementation of economic reforms. These include the needs to stabilize the foreign exchange market, explore further alternatives to privatization, revisit the role of the state, and lower the level of poverty significantly. It is also necessary to design new approaches to the domestic mobilization needed to increase savings and investment rates, ascertain external resource requirements, and lay the foundations for longer-term growth in the productive sectors, especially in agriculture and industry.

The coverage, reliability, and up to date status of economic statistics in Tanzania need to be sharply improved. A medium-term programme has been formulated to strengthen sources, coverage, and methodologies for national income accounting, particularly for such sectors as agriculture, construction, manufacturing, transport, and internal trade, and for the balance of payments. Major improvements should be made in the price data (expected to be generated) by incorporating the results of the recent household expenditure surveys. The compilation of balance of payment data will increasingly rely on more appropriatestatistical sources, particularly the use of customs data as a basis for trade-related statistics.

Experience shows that the interbank foreign exchange market needs to be restructured into a genuine interbank market in order to eliminate the undesired effects of the present structure and ensure that it is not used as conduit for capital flight. With nine commercial banks already taking part in the IFEM the desired depth and transparency are not feasible in a market limited to banks. Other issues that justify its restructuring are as follows.

(a)   There is need for improvement of accounting for export earnings. The IFEM has traded only about 25 percent of export proceeds earned during the period of its existence (to October 1995); this excludes sales by the BOT. The BOT has little information on total export proceeds received in the country. It will be easier to make commercial banks accountable on export earnings if they are relieved of the present unfair competition.

(b)   There is an increasing mismatch between the BOT's foreign exchange assets and liabilities. It will be necessary to channel some of the government payments through commercial banks, so that the BOT's intervention would serve to stabilize the market or to constitute reserves, rather than to meet immediate obligations, which tends to create panic.

(c)   The capital bases of the bureaux de change and some of the non-bank financial institutions is disproportionate to their volume of trading in the IFEM. This undermines the soundness of the financial system and imposes risk on the BOT.

(d)   There is need to eliminate bureaux de change and non-bank financial institutions from the interbank foreign exchange market, to facilitate improvement of the dealing system from the present open to a batching method and, eventually, to replace floor trading with telephone dealing, without compromising transparency and efficiency.

The recommendation is therefore to institute a genuine interbank foreign exchange market comprising only banks, which will automatically be entitled to become dealers upon obtaining a banking licence. The BOT should intervene in the market to clear excess supply and, when necessary, to meet excess demand. Whenever the BOT foreign exchange holdings are below a critical minimum requirement, the Bank should purchase foreign exchange on behalf of the government from commercial banks to meet outstanding obligations.

It follows from the foregoing discussion that the Tanzanian shilling is now floating and its rate of exchange with foreign currencies is freely determined by supply and demand in the IFEM. Contrary to expectations, the floating shilling exchange rate was relatively stable during 1994/95, depreciating by only about 15 percent in nominal terms. The advantages of a market determined exchange rate, applicable to all foreign exchange transactions in the economy, are substantial, particularly in terms of efficiency of resource allocation, and confidence building for local and foreign investors. In order to achieve the benefits of a market-based exchange system, it is important to eliminate restrictions on foreign exchange payments gradually. In other words, the principal issue with respect to exchange management in Tanzania at this stage is the extent to which movement to full convertibility of the shilling, first for current account transactions, and later for all balance of payments transactions, would affect the management of the exchange rate.

It was already known that Tanzania would accept the obligations under Article VIII of the International Monetary Fund (IMF)'s Articles of Agreement before the end of 1995. That effectively implied that to the extent that Tanzania would no longer be able to impose any restrictions on transactions of goods and services, the exchange rate would have to play the role of a shock absorber to balance changes in the supply and demand in the foreign exchange market. But the key question of whether that should be the only objective of exchange rate policy in Tanzania remained.

Exchange rate policy would have to support a competitive real exchange rate in order to promote the expansion of the competing export and import sectors. This is the only way to ensure a strong position in the balance of payments. The competitive real exchange rate that has to be defended (against appreciation) would be changing continually under the influence of various economic fundamentals, particularly technological progress and changes in relative factor productivity, net capital flows, international interest rates, etc. Thus, the central bank would periodically have to compute the real exchange rate that would constitute "the target." The second objective usually attached to exchange rate policy is to serve as a nominal anchor for low inflation, to the extent that price stability creates a favourable environment for long-term growth. However, under a floating regime, such as that already adopted by Tanzania, the exchange rate cannot be used for this purpose.

Here we should emphasize policies and measures that would enhance regional integration as an area in which Tanzania has great potential for increasing its economic growth. Moreover, the recent agreement between the Governors of the central banks of Tanzania, Uganda and Kenya on full convertibility of their currencies against each other indicates that progress can be achieved rapidly. To capitalize on Tanzania's potential, the following issues should be noted.

(a) The convertibility of the Tanzanian shilling within the region must be encouraged, with liberalization of the current account and steady movement to capital account convertibility. This would encourage development of the domestic foreign exchange market and its effective management and induce further reverse flows of leaked or externalized foreign currency by residents and non-residents, as well as encourage diversification of portfolio holdings. However, care must be taken to reduce the potential adverse effects on the money supply of permitting uncontrolled switching in and out of regional currencies.

(b) Capital account convertibility, i.e., liberalization of capital account transactions, should proceed carefully, giving due regard to issues of excess monetization and possible exchange rate upheavals. In this context, fiscal policy would need to be more restrained and responsible in such an unconstrained environment, especially because short-term effects of potential balance of payments stresses and increased interest rates would begin to bite in the early post-liberalization phase.

If the lesson of the 1970s was that the sustainability of basic needs and other socio-economic objectives was limited by a neglect of macro-structural adjustment considerations, then the lesson of the 1980s' SAPs is that focus on the latter is equally perilous unless matched by concern for the basic needs and the plight of society's vulnerable groups. While sustainable growth is necessary for the elimination of poverty, some growth patterns have a greater impact on poverty alleviation than others. Past development experiences teach us that there is a need to create an appropriate environment for the poor to increase their productivity and incomes. This could be achieved through improved access to resources and supportive public investments. This suggests that the design of development strategies in the future should be people-centred to ensure the sustainability of the development process, equity, poverty alleviation, and provision of adequate resources for human resources development. This development should be led by a growing self-reliance at all levels. In addition, future strategies should be based primarily on domestic human, financial and natural resources. Any external assistance should complement and not replace local efforts. Such external aid should be integrated into the national effort and used in the interest of the target groups for whom that assistance is meant.

The recommended growth strategy should be able to raise the income and productivity level of the poor while ensuring sustainable development. Such a growth strategy should make a dent in inequality by reducing poverty and regenerating the environment. People-centred development will require the adoption of a broad-based rural development strategy that stimulates productivity, and generates employment and incomes in both agricultural and non-agricultural activities. In a predominantly rural society like Tanzania, such a growth strategy would be consistent with the broad-based modernization of peasant agriculture. Research should pay greater attention than is presently the case to the concrete conditions and specific environment in which farmers operate, and appreciate the total farming system in which the farmer is active. In this regard, the experience of the Sasakawa Global 2000 Project stands as a solid demonstration of the great potential that exists in rural Tanzania for raising agricultural production and productivity. Under this project, the yield of maize increased from an average of 4 to 5 bags per acre to between 20 and 35 bags per acre. Sorghum yields increased from an average of 2 to 6 bags per acre to between 15 and 20 bags per acre. Wheat production at least doubled by using improved production practices through the Sasakawa Global 2000 Project. Better agricultural input procurement and distribution systems, assured marketing arrangements, and a credit system for procurement of seeds, fertilizers and equipment brought about this success. Surely, these kinds of systems and arrangements could be organized and repeated on a larger scale, hence indicating that it is feasible to implement a successful green revolution in Tanzania. The Sasakawa experience needs to be replicated all over Tanzania as part and parcel of the strategy for poverty eradication.

Development of off-farm income generating opportunities and an increase in productivity in such activities should receive high priority. In this context, emphasis should be placed on the promotion of productive public employment and rural industries. Support for small and medium size enterprises in both agriculture and industry could be effective in improving food security, generating employment and raising the level of productivity and incomes among the majority of the population. Such an approach will require supportive public investment in infrastructure, technology and marketing. The most important single infrastructural facility missing is a road network. The highest priority should be given to feeder road networks and regional roads. These should play an important role in attracting production, transport and marketing investments into the rural areas.

In pursuing macro-economic stabilization and poverty-reducing growth while pressing ahead with structural reforms, the government should continue to promote the development of an environment conducive to the creation and expansion of a strong private sector. This sector would act as the principal vehicle for growth, reduce direct government involvement in productive activities, and improve efficiency in the use of public resources. It would also enhance domestic and external competitiveness aimed at, among other things, accelerating export diversification and promoting sustainable development. Special emphasis should be placed on improving macro-economic management, particularly with respect to fiscal policy.

2. Fiscal, monetary and financial sectors

Fiscal policy issues

This chapter addresses the current status, challenges and policy options relating to fiscal policy issues, the monetary sector and financial sector reform.

Current status

Fiscal performance shows that the problems of budget overrun continue to persist. Actual total government expenditure for 1994/95 reached Tshs.491.7 billion. Out of this amount, Tshs.386.5 billion was for recurrent spending and Tshs.105.2 billion was for development. Recurrent spending indicates overruns of Tshs.13.9 billion against estimates plus supplementary expenditure approvals. The weak expenditure control system is the major cause of this budget overrun. On development spending, the actual performance has been lower than planned. It reached Tshs.105.2 billion, which is Tshs.46.3 billion less than the original estimates. This expenditure fall is largely due to lower foreign inflow for development projects.

As regards revenue, the government planned to collect Tshs.329.3 billion, or 16 percent of the GDP, during 1994/95. This amount was 35.8 percent above the 1993/94 actual revenue collection of Tshs.242.4 billion. Of this amount Tshs.301.5 billion was from taxes and Tshs.27.8 billion was from non-tax revenue. Actual performance for the year shows that total revenue reached Tshs.331.2 billion, or 16 percent of the GDP. This means the revenue target for the year was broadly attained.

Consequent to the above, the government's overall deficit (defined as domestic revenue minus total expenditure including amortization (excluding grants)) for the 1994/95 fiscal year was planned at -9.6 percent of the GDP compared to the same level reached in 1993/94. However, the overall deficit including grants was put at -3.8 percent of the GDP compared to -4.8 percent for the previous year. The overall deficit on the basis of revenue minus expenditure net of amortization (including grants) was planned at 2.8 percent of the GDP for 1994/95 compared to 2.4 percent of the GDP for 1993/94. The actual overall deficit for 1994/95 on the basis of the latter definition reached 0.7 percent of the GDP.

Financing of the 1994/95 budget deficit was covered by three sources: foreign finance of about 5.9 percent of the GDP, local non-bank borrowing of 0.3 percent of the GDP and bank borrowing of 2.7 percent of the GDP. The effect of foreign financing through borrowing has been the continued accumulation of the already substantial external debt. The huge bank borrowing figure of 2.7 percent of the GDP compared to the planned repayment of 1 percent of the GDP has made it difficult to attain one of the most important macro-economic targets of inflation reduction in 1994/95. The planned inflation target was 15 percent but it turned out to be above 20 percent. Financing the budget deficit through aid reflects dependence that calls into question the attainment of sustainability in the budget. In addition, to the extent that aid is given on the basis of conditionality and releases are contingent on many factors, it imposes an element of fragility and uncertainty on the budget.

The current fiscal position is characterized by a high expenditure to GDP ratio (of 24.1 percent) compared to a low revenue to GDP ratio (of about 16.2 percent). This has resulted in a fiscal deficit (before grants) of 7.9 percent of the GDP in the 1994/95 fiscal year. In 1995/96 the total planned expenditure was 25.4 percent of GDP while revenue expected was 18.5 percent, thus leaving a deficit of 6.9 percent of GDP. This high deficit level has called for a high level of foreign financing as well as domestic borrowing. It is the result of a weak revenue collection system (partly because of weak revenue administration) on one hand and weak enforcement of expenditure limits, resulting in government over-expenditure on the other. Despite high government expenditure compared to revenue collection, most recurrent expenditure is underfunded. A substantial portion of government expenditure has been directed to servicing external debt, meeting the wage bill, and financing defence and security requirements. This pattern of spending leaves fewer resources for other uses especially social sector requirements.

Problems and challenges

The government is facing a budgetary crisis. The existing budget structure seems to be unrealistic. The government debt service utilizes about a third of total revenue, while expenditure on other charges are budgeted to fall by about 30 percent in nominal terms and by 50 percent in real terms. Negotiations with the IMF were not concluded before December 1995 as anticipated because the IMF condition, which requires the government to attain a saving rate of at least 1.5 percent of the GDP, was not met. Moreover, balance of payments support from bilateral donors, particularly Nordic countries, will not be forthcoming for some time to come. As the 1995/96 budget estimated a deficit of Tshs.172 billion, it is obvious that this was a tough budget since the amounts provided would not satisfy demands, hence underfunding of some operations may have increased even further.

Expenditure control has proved elusive for the following reasons:

(a)   discussion between the Treasury and the ministries on the budgetary estimates in order to determine expenditure priorities and the adequacy of funding for priority activities jointly has been given insufficient attention

(b) the wage bill includes a wide range of allowances which, because of the difficulty of unifying them across ministries, have invariably resulted in unplanned increases in components of the compensation package

(c) domestic debt service expenditure has been difficult to determine because of uncertainties about the size of the fiscal deficit

(d) the provision that allows ministries to transfer funds across items within votes has tended to generate excess expenditure in the perceived priority areas, and

(e) discipline has been lacking in the budget process itself, particularly when there are inadequate links between expenditures and available resources.

All these are challenges or problems that the third phase government will have to address. Towards the end of 1994/95, the government took steps aimed at improving the mechanisms of expenditure control. These steps included limiting the level of monthly revenue releases to ministries by the Treasury through the Bank of Tanzania to an amount based on the monthly average of revenue collected during the previous three months. The government has also placed "account examiners" from the Ministry of Finance (MOF) in key ministries to certify that the ministries' accounts have a positive balance before funds for expenditures are committed and cheques are issued.

Financing government expenditure by the sale of Treasury Bills (T-bills) is not sustainable, as this will increase interest rates, which may discourage productive investment since prospective investors will invest in T-bills. The sale of T-bills may also cause banks to push up interest rates to enable them to compete in order to attract deposits. Increase in interest rates would also worsen the debt service obligation.

On the revenue side some measures, such as the one to reduce custom duties on imported food stuffs including rice, sugar, cooking oil and wheat, may act against the goal of protecting domestic agriculture in order to attain food self sufficiency. This, for example, may in turn reduce government tax revenue collection and may not necessarily be passed on to consumers in the form of low prices. On the contrary, it may just increase the rents of those importers that were previously paying higher taxes.

Tax evasion is one of the problems that reduce tax yields. The challenge is to enhance revenue collection while simultaneously bringing government spending under control. Tax evasion has continued to be a big problem despite tax rates being reduced beginning in 1986, and pre-shipment inspection and customs duty collection being handled by "experienced" companies such as Société Générale de Surveillance and Cotecna Inspection S.A. Tanzania.

One of the constraints on tax administration in Tanzania has been the complexity and, in some cases, the weakness, of tax laws and overall tax structure. Some of the laws are not open to a clear interpretation or have been abused (e.g., law on tax exemption) to the detriment of overall tax administration and revenue collection. The complexity of the structure with too many taxes and rate categorization has also exerted enormous administrative demands that are not easily met given the lack of skilled manpower and other resource constraints. Lenient tax laws and penalties have also encouraged evasion and avoidance of taxes, since most laws which stipulate penalties, especially monetary penalties, have not been frequently updated in accordance with the changes in the value of money and thus over time have become non-deterrent.

Poor and inconsistent records constitute another problem that makes administration and tax revenue collection difficult. Because of inadequate skilled staff and working facilities, various tax departments, especially the Income Tax and Sales Tax Departments, have not been able to identify each individual taxpayer. Even when some taxpayers are identified, however, all trace has usually been lost due to poor record-keeping resulting from a lack of modern record-keeping facilities and the non-existence of a system of numbers or master filing. Moreover, vital exchange of information about taxpayers between various departments that would enable cross-checking of this information, for example between Income Tax and Sales Tax Departments, has been lacking. Thus a large number of potential taxpayers escape the scrutiny of the tax departments, especially the Sales Tax Department. A proposal to have a computerized taxpayer identification system has been around for a long time without being acted upon. About 70 percent of government tax revenues originate from Dar es Salaam, thus it should be relatively easy to establish such a taxpayer identification system within six months for Dar es Salaam. The system could be linked with other identification systems (customs duty, income tax, sales tax, company registration, voter registration, social security etc). Corrupt income tax, customs duty, and sales tax officials do not like this system because it would prevent them from getting easy bribes.

Policy options

Budget structure
In order to ensure that essential government services are fully funded, it is important that budgetary estimates from ministries are thoroughly discussed

with the Treasury so as to jointly determine priority activities and to agree on the amounts of funding that would adequately cover them. There is need to ensure adequate time for thorough discussions of ministerial budgets, and in order to ensure that budgetary discussions are comprehensive and rigorous it is recommended that preparations for the next year's budget commence in October. An analysis of the budget passed by Parliament during the June-August Parliamentary Budget Session should be followed by the budget's preparation. Some of the problems with the current budgeting process are due to insufficient time spent in preparing the government budget. This process should be more-or-less continuous. Some mini-budgets have occurred because of rushed preparation and inadequate analysis of the impact of proposed measures, for example, tax incidence, revenue impact analysis, tax buoyancy, etc.

To eliminate underbudgeting, procedural changes should be made to ensure that budgetary discussions are comprehensive and rigorous, requiring strict adherence to the official budgetary timetable. To ensure that ministries spend funds as budgeted, the government should repeal the provision in the Financial Orders which allows an accounting officer to transfer funds across items within a vote or sub-vote without prior authorization from the Treasury.

The monitoring of budgetary performance should be strengthened by a rigorous and continuous scrutiny by the Comptroller and Auditor General to ensure that shortcomings and irregularities in fiscal implementation are brought swiftly to the attention of the Ministry of Finance.

Expenditure
Deficit reduction requires not only an increase in tax revenue collection but also an effective control of government spending. Major actors in the budget process (the Parliament, Ministry of Finance, the Auditor General, the Bank of Tanzania, the Planning Commission, and donors) are well placed to ensure this. Obviously, reduction or effective control of government expenditure requires budgetary discipline and a sound budgeting system. In turn, a sound budgeting system calls for proper expenditure forecasting, sharp monitoring of expenditures, and strict enforcement of expenditure limits. Over-expenditure of the budgeted funds needs to be avoided, and where absolutely necessary it should, before being undertaken by the spending units, be approved by Parliament. Likewise, the practice of submitting mini-budgets must be avoided.

The principal objectives of expenditure policies over the medium-term are to:

(a)   reduce the role of the government in direct productive activities

(b)   limit the activities that the government undertakes in order to focus scarce resources on high priority areas

(c)   increase expenditures on basic health care, primary education, and water and sewerage, and

(b)   improve expenditure-control systems.

In order for the new government to come up with a meaningful budget it is necessary to:

(a)   restrain the growth of public debt, both local and foreign, in the budget to ensure having adequate resources for normal government operations

(b)   initiate discussions with both bilateral and multilateral donors, with the aim of requesting a substantial cancellation of the debt burden

(c)   examine the existing structure of the government with the aim of establishing a more viable and optimal structure, and

(d)   enforce financial regulations at all levels to ensure budgetary discipline. Expenditure overrun beyond the authorized levels has been facilitated by lack of enforcement of disciplinary actions, particularly from top leadership.

Government pay structure is characterized by a number of weaknesses that lead to complaints from almost all cadres and professionals as well as difficulties in the management of the wage bill. There is need for the government to examine and rationalize the current government pay structure aimed at enhancing efficiency in the public sector.

Revenue

To improve tax administration and collection, the government has established the Tanzania Revenue Authority (TRA). This will be the central body for assessing and collecting government's principal revenues, as well as for administering and enforcing the laws with respect to revenue collection. The authority will also be responsible for the establishment, maintenance, and application of a taxpayer identification system. This system will be aimed at controlling tax evasion by requiring taxpayers to maintain proper business records for purposes of tax audit, and by ensuring that taxpayers do not fail to file returns. One of the immediate tasks of the new government is to make the TRA operational. To ensure that the government's principal revenues are dealt with efficiently, the following requirements should be taken into account.

(a)   There is a need to improve the recording and strengthening of information about taxpayers, e.g., exchange of information between various tax departments. The TRA can facilitate this procedure.

(b) There is a need to activate the integration of revenue collection. At present, revenue collection falls under two categories: collection of earmarked revenue (user charges such as fees, tolls, etc., collected by education, health, and public works ministries), and collection of non-earmarked revenue (taxes, royalties, etc., collected by the Treasury through the tax department and other line ministries, etc.). The third phase government should integrate the collection of these two types of revenue to increase efficiency. In order to enhance collection of these types of revenue, the third phase government should:

(i) ensure the existence of a strong and efficient collection machinery in the ministries, regions and other institutions, and

(ii) provide adequate supporting facilities, including the right type of manpower to strengthen revenue management (through revenue forecasting, setting appropriate rates of fees and collection), in these institutions.

(c) There is a need to improve the tax collection system, which can be achieved through modernization of tax collection procedures and by a broadening of the tax base. The use of modern working instruments such as vehicles, calculators, computers, etc. would lead to greater efficiency. Rationalization of the institutional structure of the present revenue authority is also called for. There are presently four revenue departments and one head office. These should include the staff requirement for the authority to function effectively. However, it is quite obvious that the present structure is over-staffed. Once the TRA is effectively established there will also be a need for the government to reconsider the presence of the pre-shipment inspection companies with a view to terminating their services.

There are substantial areas of uncollected revenue running into billions of shillings. This is in respect of all types of taxes, import taxes as well as domestic taxes. Some sources put the estimated arrears of revenue at Tshs.24 billion. Apart from arrears on tax revenue, the government has also failed to collect substantial amounts of arrears on import support funds. Efforts to collect these funds will considerably improve the government budget. The new government should design workable machinery that will ensure that arrears of revenue and commodity import support are collected.

There are weaknesses in the collection of taxes on transit trade to neighbouring countries and on goods coming to the mainland through Zanzibar. Those who are involved in transit trade have been evading taxes by redirecting non taxable goods meant for neighbouring countries to the domestic market. Similarly, goods from Zanzibar which have either been taxed at lower rates or not taxed at all in Zanzibar have found their way into the Mainland thus denying the Union government its tax revenue, as well as causing unfair competition with domestically produced goods. The new government must come up with a very strong tax administration that will ensure effective control of transit trade and goods coming from Zanzibar.

(d)   The tax base should be broadened. The third phase government must design an appropriate agricultural tax policy for both domestic and export crops to broaden the tax base without discouraging production or exports. In the decade of the 1970s direct taxes, particularly on export crops, were very high and contributed substantially to government revenue. After concerted criticism, the government learnt its lesson too well—it quickly moved to abolish taxes on agriculture altogether. It is high time the government reconsiders this policy. It may well be that what was needed from the beginning was a substantial reduction rather than complete removal of direct taxes on agricultural crops. A way should also be sought of taxing small scale miners, transporters, coffee auctions and small businesses.

(e)   Voluntary compliance among taxpayers should be encouraged, and this can be achieved by lowering tax rates to motivate people to pay tax, spending tax money properly as opposed to misusing it, providing tax education, and introducing tax identities and a tax register. More broadly, there is need to re-examine the system of tax assessment, the tax payment period, the system of staggering tax payments, penalties, fines and other punitive measures against tax evaders, tax payment arrears, etc. Stiff jail sentences and confiscation or expropriation of a tax evader's wealth and/or property will be a strong deterrent. Tax administration can on the other hand be improved by paying tax collectors and administrators well, and through the use of modern working tools, etc.

(f)   Another way in which the tax base can be broadened is by reducing exemptions. It is obvious that tax exemption has been the major cause of erosion of the tax base in the country. The outgoing government was known for granting generous exemptions to taxpayers. The new government must examine seriously the type and nature of tax exemptions in existence with a view to substantially reducing them.

(g)   The 'right' macro-economic policies should be implemented to ensure a buoyant economy.

(h)   The tax system should be streamlined by simplifying and updating various tax laws, reducing tax rate categorizations, and abolishing unimportant taxes.

Monetary sector

Current status

After the passing of the new Bank of Tanzania Act, 1995, the Bank has moved away from multiple policy objectives to a single goal: price stability. On the basis of empirical evidence, which suggests that inflation is mainly caused by the excessive creation of money, the Bank of Tanzania has begun the task of regulating the quantity of money in circulation and the credit supplied to the economy. To achieve this objective, the Bank formulates and implements monetary policy using such instruments as discounting policy, minimum reserve policy, open market policy, foreign exchange interventions, etc.

Despite the policy efforts made on the monetary front, the growth of M3[3] has still been high, mainly because of a rapid expansion in the net claims on the government by the banking system, particularly the BOT, as well as increased net foreign exchange holdings by commercial banks. Lending to the government is, for example, the main reason behind non-attainment of the monetary programme in 1994/95—an indication that there is more need for emphasis on strict fiscal policy in pursuit of price stability.

Some other measures that have been taken at the start of 1995/96 to ensure the attainment of the set targets include: requiring the NBC and the Cooperative Rural Development Bank (CRDB) to freeze their lending at the end of June 1995 levels; limiting the BOT's discount policy only to Treasury Bills so as to limit commercial bank access to Bank credit and promote an interbank market in local currency; and increasing the use of Treasury Bill operations and foreign exchange interventions to manage liquidity. As mentioned above, the success of the 1995/96 financial programme will depend heavily on the sound implementation of fiscal policy, resulting in the repayment of Tshs.50.5 billion to the BOT. The resources released by the government could sufficiently meet the credit requirements of the private sector for the financing of production, without creating pressure of liquidity expansion in the economy. Contrary to expectations, by the end of August 1995 the stock of M3 had grown to Tshs.691.9 billion (or by 8 percent from its June 30, 1995 level), exceeding the end of September 1995 target by Tshs.31.8 billion. Once again, the main cause of the rapid expansion in the stock of M3 during July and August 1995 was net credit to the government, which rose by Tshs.23 billion.

At the present time, due to the large and sustained fiscal disequilibrium financed through bank borrowing and Treasury Bill auctions, serious monetary imbalances exist and are the causes of instability in the financial markets. Market-determined interest rates, such as deposit and lending rates, are not only misaligned with the Treasury Bill yield rates but are also not responsive to changes in policy-related rates, i.e., the discount rates. The absence of a benchmark rate, which should have been the Treasury Bill yield rates, is the result of the excessive need to finance the government, using Treasury Bills, and the lack of depth, competition, and efficacy in the financial sector. The auctioning of Treasury Bills has tended to deny the productive sectors of investment credit and its upward push of interest rates has diverted resources from productive investments to speculative activities and other quick-yielding investments in activities such as trade. Treasury Bills auctions were introduced with a view to mopping up excess liquidity and sterilizing it in blocked accounts. In re-examining the functioning of Treasury Bills auctions this original objective should also be borne in mind. Once again the problem of Treasury Bills being used as speculative investment is tied to the problem of inflation. So long as inflation is at double-digit levels, investors will tend to engage in speculative investment.

The requirement under the financial sector reform programme that non-creditworthy parastatals would not be granted credit and that existing facilities would be terminated meant a drop in credit to state sector entities and an increase in the volume of credit to the private sector. For instance, between June 1991 and June 1994 commercial bank credit to state sector entities declined from Tshs.106.9 billion to Tshs.97.1 billion while credit to the private sector increased from Tshs.41.0 billion to Tshs.158.9 billion.[4] The consequence of this redistribution of credit meant that public enterprises in manufacturing activity faced a shortage of working capital while private sector activity, mostly in trade and commerce, received an increased allocation of credit (for working capital).

Outstanding problems and challenges

Among the outstanding problems and challenges in the sector are the following.

Containment of fiscal deficit

The main constraint in the pursuit of price stability in the country is, first and foremost, the large budget deficit arising from undisciplined fiscal policies. Financing of the deficit through domestic sources is a cause of serious monetary imbalances and has brought about instability in the financial markets. The use of Treasury Bills to generate the required financing:

(a) may be the cause of high interest rates, worsening the domestic debt servicing burden, as efforts by the BOT to lower such costs through setting a cut-off price are likely to result in the curtailment of demand for the many bills, and thus to conflict with the desire to mop up liquidity

(b) denies the BOT a key instrument in liquidity management, and

(c) has, given its attractive yields, steered away credit from the productive sectors and the private sector—a clear manifestation of the "crowding-out effect".

Efficacy of monetary policy instruments

Monetary policy should aim at achieving and sustaining a low rate of inflation consistent with overall growth and balance of payments objectives. It has been observed above that for quite some time, the monetary and inflationary targets have been at wide variance with actual performance. This is not only due to a lack of fiscal discipline but also to the ineffectiveness of some instruments used to control the expansion of money. In this regard, there is a need to phase out direct instruments and emphasize effective use of indirect monetary policy instruments, which are reputed to have a firmer grip.

Policy options

Containment of the fiscal disequilibrium

Improved fiscal performance is a necessary condition for improved liquidity management, the development of efficient financial markets, and the promotion of price stability. Given that it is not easy to correct the fiscal deficit on a sustainable basis unless structural issues pertaining to revenue collection and expenditure control are addressed, both of which will take time, the following initial steps need to be taken immediately.

(a) The government should improve fiscal discipline as a condition for improved liquidity management, the development of an efficient money market, and the promotion of price stability. This will entail improved coordination at the technical as well as policy level.

(b) In order to ensure that fiscal discipline is maintained, a cash budget system (which entails the balancing of expenditure to the available resources) needs to be strengthened. Such a system will eliminate the possibility of government borrowing from the banking system or the market. It is important to stress here that promotion of price stability through strict management of the budget needs commitment from the authorities and the general public after they have been made aware of the evils of inflation. The success of the cash-budgeting system in controlling expenditures should be coupled with aggressive measures to raise revenue so that the government is capable of utilizing the budgeted expenditure levels. To effect this, the Tanzania Revenue Authority should be made operational as soon as possible. The revenue leakage channels also need to be closed as quickly as possible.

Financial sector reforms
Institutional development in the financial sector (i.e., the creation of money and capital markets) is required in order to boost the efficacy of monetary policy. To achieve this effect it is recommended that:

(a)   the information flow to and from the market is increased
(b)   the restructuring of financial institutions is continued in order to improve efficiency and quality of assets
(c)   existing and new financial instruments are popularized, and
(d)   a secondary market for both money and capital market instruments is developed and the establishment of the stock exchange is facilitated.

Strengthening the institutional framework
There is a need to strengthen the institutional framework for macro-economic management by putting in place effective machinery for consultation and policy coordination between the Ministry of Finance, the Planning Commission, and the Bank of Tanzania. Such an institutional framework would enable monetary policy to be properly coordinated with other economic policies thereby ensuring that price stability is restored. It is therefore recommended that:

(a)   the Monetary Policy Committee (MPC) meet more regularly, i.e., once every month
(b)   a Technical Committee of the MPC be set up, which should meet weekly to oversee the implementation of the decisions made by MPC
(c)   the Macro-economic Group Committee should be strengthened and regularized, and
(d)   within the institutions, there should be special units assigned to monitor the implementation of the economic programmes.

Financial sector reforms

Current status

The present financial structure in Tanzania is a result of reforms and liberalization of the formal financial sector started in the mid-1980s. The aims of reforms and liberalization have been:

(a)   to establish a framework for a healthy and competitive banking system
(b)   to restrict and refinance the formal financial intermediaries in order to clean up the balance sheets of the state owned banks and financial institutions
(c)   to liberalize the foreign exchange market so as to eliminate the pre-reform restrictions on the holding, transactions and transfer of foreign currency
(d)   to establish a capital market and securities authority for promoting and facilitating the development of an orderly, fair, efficient capital market and securities industry in the country
(e)   to enact and implement a law that allows more independence of the central bank to foster sound banking principles and maintain price stability, and
(f)   to deregulate the depository and lending interest rates and adopt a market-oriented interest rate policy which allows financial institutions to determine their own lending rates at a level below the given maximum.

There is no doubt that all these measures demonstrate the seriousness on the part of the government to provide for a commercially based and autonomous financial sector marked by prudent regulation of financial activities in a market-oriented economic regime. As an indication of a positive response to the reform measures a number of domestic and foreign private commercial banks and other financial intermediaries have been issued with temporary or permanent licenses to operate in the country since 1991.

A study of financial sector reform has given further insights into options of reform. The major components of financial sector reform as proposed by the report of the Presidential Banking Commission (1990) are: the enactment of new banking and financial institutions legislation; enhancing the autonomy of banks; and enhancing competition and free entry into the financial sector. Major institutional changes in the Tanzanian financial landscape have included the establishment of the Capital Markets and Securities Authority (CMSA) in 1994 and the establishment of private sector banks and other financial institutions. The high minimum deposits required by these new banks and their exclusive location in Dar es Salaam suggests that these banks have so far targeted corporate deposits and deposits from high income groups in urban areas rather than catered for the needs of the low income earners in urban and rural areas. The institutional developments of the capital markets are still in their infancy. The securities market is still confined to government securities.

Following the reforms and liberalization of the financial sector the old regulated financial sector, which was marked by tightly controlled interest rates, credit ceilings and direct allocations, and limited entry into banking, has been eliminated. These reforms and those in other sectors of the economy have produced modest but encouraging results. The net domestic savings mobilized and investment have, for example, been on the increase in nominal terms since 1989. Similarly, the reform period has been characterized by encouraging, though below target, positive real rates of growth.

Challenges

The achievements so far notwithstanding, there are certain issues that still pose a challenge to policy formation.

(a)   The failure of or non-orientation of new financial intermediaries to lend to small-scale borrowers or to mobilize savings from the small potential savers in rural and urban areas is a problem. Most of the operations of these institutions are guided by the traditional commercial banking ethics, which emphasize short-term lending. It appears that the new private banks have not targeted new market niches but only entered into competition with the local commercial banks, particularly the NBC, which dominates short-term lending and mobilization of savings in the economy. All the nine financial intermediaries that have emerged after the adoption of reforms are headquartered in Dar es Salaam. A likely trend is that the branch networks of the new foreign banks will be expanded into the commercial urban centres and only those in the middle and high-income brackets will directly benefit from the liberalization of the financial sector.

(b)   The high lending rates mean that an increasing number of borrowers are unable to obtain loans from commercial banks at the going rates and borrowing conditions.

(c)   Weak supervision of the financial system and thefts within the banks, especially the NBC, serve to destabilize the financial system and undermine the entire exercise of recapitalizing the state owned banks. Such a lack of supervision may erode the confidence of the public in the banks.

Thus, in spite of the reforms and the liberalization of the financial sector, the financial structure is still ineffective and inefficient in attending to the reforms in other sectors, which would in turn trigger economic growth and development.

Tanzania can draw lessons from the financial reform efforts of other countries. Reviewing the experiences of Latin America (the Southern Cone) it has been shown that complete deregulation of financial operations and transactions undermined stabilization efforts and led to financial instability and speculation. This contrasts with the Asian model where liberalization allowed for more lead-time, was more gradual and recognized the need for control of the banking system. Lessons drawn from these experiences are that abrupt and full-scale liberalization tends to destabilize the financial system while properly monitored deregulation tends to be more successful. A high degree of flexibility and adaptability to changing circumstances contributed to the success of the Asian model.

Fragmentation of the financial markets and the dualism in these markets reflect the dualism that is characteristic of the real sector. However, market segmentation per se does not necessarily imply inefficient intermediation. In the Asian model, success resulted from the creation of conditions that allow the growth and evolution of individual segments of the financial markets and for the development of effective linkages among these markets. In a number of Asian countries, the interlining of contracts across financial, trade and production transactions and layering of credit have been used for risk management by informal lenders in the rural areas. These techniques have facilitated information gathering and contract enforcement.

One important lesson for Tanzania is that efforts should be made to achieve closer integration of the formal and informal financial markets. Enhancing the interactive mechanisms to reduce the operational constraints facing each market while capitalizing on the strength of each market could do this. There may be several other ways of achieving integration such as: introducing into formal financial markets some elements of the flexibility of informal markets; strengthening the structure and performance of informal markets; or developing linkages between formal and informal financial markets.

The prerequisites for successful financial liberalization (macro-economic stability and a working regulatory and supervisory framework) are difficult to establish or sustain. The design of the financial reforms should take into account sequencing and the speed of deepening in financial markets in changing macro-economic conditions. Policies should be flexibly designed to cope with changing circumstances.

The development of financial intermediation is critically dependent on improvements in monitoring, evaluation and enforcement. These underline the importance of creating and strengthening a market-supporting infrastructure for financial sector development. This includes measures to strengthen the legal infrastructure and measures to enhance the information capital base, which reduce the cost of acquiring reliable information.

Policy options

Short-term policy options
Among the short-term policy options are the needs to:

(a) adopt a policy on interest rates which allows for a modest degree of financial repression in order to allow for growth in investment, so that in this respect, in the short run the ceilings and floors on the saving and lending rates are maintained at some given minimum levels rather than eliminated

(b) accommodate a policy that emphasizes further broadening of the financial sector, in particular one that allows institution of new financial intermediaries especially in areas of the country which are disadvantaged but have good potential for investment

(c) put in place short-term policy measures under which the cash reserve and statutory liquidity ratios are reduced (rather than increased) in phases in order to allow the growth stimuli in the economy to develop

(d) put in place a well supported inspectorate arm to overcome regulatory and supervisory shortcomings that have emerged in the short period of financial reforms in the country, and strengthen the Central Bank's supervision directorate and related procedures

(e) reform and liberalize the insurance sector to allow private insurance operators and increase the number of sectors and instruments served, and

(f) foster an environment for capital growth and attend to remaining institutional bottlenecks that impede the growth of capital and money markets, which so far are yet to emerge as important sources of finance in the country.

The government should ensure that rules concerning the capital adequacy of the banks and other financial institutions are strictly observed. However, to allow for the emergence of more non-bank financial institutions (NBFIs), the minimum initial capital amounts set for the potential local financial institutions may need to be revised downwards. As a short-term policy option NBFIs could also be legalized to select a portfolio selection which is not solely constituted of Treasury Bonds as is the current practice. In other words, NBFIs should be legally allowed to invest in financial instruments other than the low interest bearing government bonds and costly real estate in order to increase the supply of long-term finance to the private sector.

In addition, the government must encourage the banks to recover debts and the interest thereof speedily. The practice that has been followed by the banks is that of indicating unreceived interest on assets as income. However, it might be better for the banks to adopt an accounting system under which they report interest income only if and when received. In the intermittent period, the banks will, however, be required to pay interest on deposits. Therefore, their profits will only be reported if the banks have collected substantial interest on the loans disbursed. If this policy is adopted it is likely that the recycling of the mobilized savings would be enhanced.

It is also important to make credit available to the key economic sectors and the poor who have limited access to financial resources. In this context, it is imperative that the government make a concerted effort in order to supply low priced (concessionary) credit to the disadvantaged sectors and groups by combining both short-term policy measures, including interest rates, and subsidized credit.

Long-term policy options
The long-term policy options include the following.

(a) There is a need to create an environment in which banks will have better incentives to lend more to agriculture, small-scale enterprises and other priority sectors. In this case, particular efforts could be directed to revival of abandoned agricultural credit institutions and perfection and facilitation of the smooth operation of agricultural produce marketing institutions, agencies and individual traders. The government should facilitate the development of rural financial markets which in turn could encourage the establishment of community-based intermediaries with savings mobilization and allocation and payments functions, while at the same time creating opportunities for banks and other financial institutions to extend their services to the rural sector.

(b) For the sake of bolstering its capacity and effectively serving financial intermediation in the economy, it is important that legally recognized and defined links between the formal and informal financial sectors are allowed and facilitated. Owing to the inadequacies of the formal financial sector, an increasing number of borrowers and savers have taken refuge in the informal financial sector. The formal-informal financial sector link can become efficient if Non Governmental Organizations (NGOs) are legally authorized to operate as quasi-financial intermediaries which would be able to engage in mobilizing savings needed to bolster their lending capacity to targeted and even untargeted groups in their areas of operation. The success story of Kenya's Rural Enterprises Programme (KREP) serves to justify the formal-semi-formal link as a promising way in which the existing financial institutions may act in the period of reforms.

(c) The government should continue to be committed to improving the efficiency of financial intermediation. Restructuring and privatization of public sector banks should be accorded high priority. As a further step to facilitate increased competition in the financial system, the government should continue, selectively, to encourage the entry of new banking institutions into Tanzania. In the medium to long-term period, efforts should be directed to the deepening of the financial structure by encouraging the development of new financial institutions, instruments and markets. In this regard there is a need to establish financial institutions (companies and merchant banks) which will participate in the broader financial market. These would also serve many of the small business enterprises that are mostly family-oriented and are, as already highlighted, incapable of borrowing from the banks. They would also foster competition and offer more financial instruments to savers and investors.

3.   Productive sectors

This chapter addresses the current status of the productive sectors, identifies the main challenges and proposes policy options. The productive sectors that are examined here are agriculture, mining and industry.

Agriculture sector

Current status

Agriculture is the foundation of the Tanzanian economy, underpinning employment, food production and exports. The agricultural sector, which is comprised of crops, animal husbandry, fishery and hunting sub-sectors, continues to be the dominant sector in the economy. Some 80 percent of the total employed population are in agriculture. Overall, the agricultural sector accounts for over 40 percent of the GDP and 75 percent of total foreign exchange earnings.

The largest share of foreign exchange earnings is derived from traditional export crops, which include coffee, cotton, cashew nut, pyrethrum, tea, tobacco and sisal. Export crops, however, account for a small share of the sector's output. Agricultural production is still based on traditional technologies: the hand-hoe, limited application of modern farm inputs and irrigation. Agricultural crop production is still dominated by peasant farmers (about 3,692,328) most of whom work small family holdings. The average cultivated area is 0.9 ha. and some 93 percent of all farmers cultivate less than 2.0 ha.

Since the 1980s, a wide range of policies and institutional reforms at the macro and sectoral levels has affected the agricultural sector. The economic reform measures took cognizance of the agricultural sector as the engine of economic growth and development. In particular, currency devaluation and liberalization of both crop marketing and distribution of inputs have been practised with a view to increasing the prices and the volume of the food and traditional export crops. Associated with these policy reform measures in the rest of the economy has been the removal of subsidies on farm inputs and to the crop marketing parastatals.

A major objective of the recent economic recovery programme has been to stimulate agricultural output by increasing producer incentives and hence improving agriculture's terms of trade. The reforms adopted have been instrumental in reversing the poor performance of the agricultural sector experienced in the pre-reform period because:

(a)   the competitive crop marketing system has enabled producers to retain a larger share of the f.o.b. export price. although this share is still below the set target of 70 percent

(b) complete liberalization of food crop marketing has led to competition and increased speculation by producers for better prices through holding stocks, which enhances the food security objective of ensuring availability of food throughout the year at affordable prices, and

(c) the increase in producer prices and the liberalized marketing of crops has led to a rise in the use of fertilizer, hybrid seeds, and other productivity enhancing technologies in the high potential agricultural areas.

Substantial increase in crop output during the reform period has, however, only been recorded in the production of food crops (staple cereals). The recovery of agricultural exports has been less phenomenal. As a result, the performance of the agriculture sector during the past three years was less satisfactory. The share of agriculture in real GDP grew by 2.3 percent in 1992, increased to 7.3 percent in 1993, then dropped by 2 percent in 1994.

Some of the reasons for the unsatisfactory performance of agriculture over the past three years were: inadequate and unreliable supply of major inputs, coupled with poor distribution; unfavourable world market prices; poor extension services coupled with vulnerable research services on different crops; dilapidated ginneries; erratic rains; and poor transportation and communication networks in the country which was again aggravated by deteriorating roads, railway trucks and wagons to ferry crops and inputs. However, it is likely that the delayed participation of the private sector in the procurement and exporting of crops and the delayed reform of the crop parastatals continued to adversely influence returns to farmers, and consequently undermine their incentive to increase output.

Along with declines in agricultural productivity and marketed output, processing capacities for agricultural crops (such as coffee, tea, cashew nut, sugar, sisal) and sugar processing facilities have suffered. Persistent under-utilization of capacity contributes to high processing costs, which eat into the farmer's share of the export price.

Recent studies indicate that poverty in Tanzania is overwhelmingly a rural problem. Poverty in the rural areas is directly linked to low output and productivity in the agricultural sector. This can largely be explained by continued predominance of poor agricultural technologies used by the farmers, limited use of fertilizer, etc. In addition, agriculture in Tanzania continues to be dependent on the whims of nature: drought, floods, etc. The latter factors, together with variation in soil fertility, have also accounted for the existence of regional inequality in the country. The recovery of the agricultural sector and the economy in general seems to have benefited the rural population inequitably. A tentative conclusion is that rural income inequality is increasing.

Total government expenditure as a share of the GDP rose from about 23.1 percent in 1986/87 to 26.4 percent in 1991/92; but the largest share went mainly to finance the losses of parastatals. In 1990 for example, spending on parastatals represented 37.1 percent of the development expenditure of the Ministry of Agriculture. While this percentage has continued to be high, the crop parastatals also continued to benefit from exemptions on paying taxes and import support counter funds. Furthermore, these parastatals continue to be allowed to default on commercial loans from the banks, etc.

The share of government expenditure committed to agriculture declined from 4.9 percent in 1991/92 to 4.2 percent in 1994/95. As a result, essential extension and research services declined in both quantity and quality. Many workers in these institutions have remained ill equipped and unmotivated given the precipitous decline in their real wages (along with other workers in government).

Reforms of both research and extension services proposed by the government are still largely on the drawing board. The situation is pathetic as the little research being done hardly reaches the farmer partly because the extension agents have almost no contact with him.

The agricultural sector has only managed to attract a very small proportion of formal commercial credit for crop production. With the decline in the importance of parastatals and cooperatives in crop purchases and input distribution, the share of bank credit going to finance these activities has also declined. Some of this credit remained in the sector by going to newer uses in the agricultural sector, notably for export of non-traditional agricultural products. However, the change generally represented a loss to other sectors like trade, which had hitherto been marginalized by the huge requirements of the marketing parastatals and cooperatives.

The government has pulled away from the subsidization of agricultural inputs. In view of the increases in input prices after the adoption of economic reforms, the need for more credit facilities to assist the farmer to purchase these inputs is even greater. Studies show that there are informal channels of credit operating in the country. There are also saving credit associations, NGOs, etc. that serve financial needs in the rural areas. However, such informal finance sources cannot be left on their own to take care of all the production and agricultural development needs of the farmer. Some way must be found of extending formal credit to the farmers.

Issues and challenges

In order for the agricultural sector to continue supplying the food and foreign exchange needed by a self-sustaining growing economy, it is imperative that the sector grow at an even faster pace. This is also important in order to address the issue of poverty and its alleviation since, as noted above, poverty in Tanzania is predominantly a rural problem. The above current status review of agriculture has already alluded to the outstanding problems and challenges in the sector. These problems can briefly be put into two categories, namely problems relating to the sector in general and those that are related to specific crops.

General problems of the agricultural sector include:

(a)   inadequate attention to extension and research as a consequence of many years of underfunding these services
(b)   the low level of technology used in Tanzanian agriculture, including the ecological considerations that must be made in improving this technology
(c)   the problems of deforestation and land degradation caused by over-cultivation and over-grazing under low levels of technology
(d)   disease and pest epidemics, as there is need to develop concerted efforts to deal with these problems in a systematic way to avoid recurring costly epidemics and eventually to eliminate the problems altogether
(e)   the lack of credit facilities earmarked for the specific needs of the sector, as credit is needed both by farmers and traders in crops and inputs, and some traders have withdrawn from trade in inputs because of lack of credit to finance their input supply operations, and
(f)   land cultivated by the farmers which, as in most cases, is still held on a traditional tenure basis thus reducing private investment and farmers' access to bank because such land cannot be used as collateral security.

In view of the fact that Tanzania will have to depend mainly on its own farmers for cereals (rice and maize) there is need to look at the sustainability of cereal production at various levels of technology. There are regions that have exhausted all the land suitable for production of cereals using low technology production systems. In Dodoma, Kilimanjaro, and Singida marginal lands are already being brought into production. There are some regions that can allow land to lie fallow without having to exhaust high potential land, even with low technology. In all areas, however, including these, reduced fallow is related to the problem of increased land degradation. With improved technology, land can be used more intensively. This will conserve good potential land while raising productivity and incomes.

Some crops are becoming less profitable to the farmer in terms of returns to labour. Often this is due to the increased labour needed or the rising cost of inputs. As a result, farmers are switching to more attractive crops. Research can help to produce varieties that are more resistant to plant diseases and labour saving technology can make some crops more attractive to the farmer. Meanwhile, non-traditional export crops, for example oil seeds and sesame, have become quite competitive relative to the traditional export crops. Production of such crops needs to be expanded.

Liberalization of the crop marketing system has elicited some efficiency. However, the increased participation of the private sector in crop marketing has meant that the government's job of monitoring the sector through the collection of information about production, prices, and marketing has increased in magnitude and importance. Liberalization has also brought some specific problems to this sector. A regulatory framework is needed to ensure consistent product quality. The marked increases in marketed output in the food sub-sector that have followed liberalization are threatened because of the lack of a regulatory framework to enable the participation of the private sector and facilitate its use of crop processing facilities still owned by the parastatals and the cooperative movement. The effect of liberalization has made production of cereals nearer consumption centres more profitable and that in the distant southern zone, which comprises of Rukwa, Songea and Mbeya, less profitable. Inter-regional trade in cereals with neighbouring countries may hold the key to sustained output in the southern zone.

The government needs to study both short and long-term problems and prospects confronting individual crops/categories of crops in order to determine the appropriate strategies to pursue. Coffee and cotton yields and sales have been affected by particular problems. There has been a recent drastic fall in coffee world markets on the one hand and on the other an increase in the adverse impact of coffee leaf rust and coffee berry diseases. The development of disease resistant strains is crucial in order to lower production costs in view of the poor economic prospects in the international economy. Meanwhile, the increase in the default and evasion of marketing regulations accompanying the liberalization of cotton marketing has increased the spread of cotton diseases and has diminished the reliability and adequacy of cotton-seed supplies.

However, for certain other crops the prospects are good, providing particular steps are taken to improve their yields and accessibility.

(a) The planting of more new trees and the improvement of agronomic practices will contribute to further increases in cashew nut output.

(b) Improved husbandry practices and afforestation to replenish fuel-wood supply hold the key to sustained tobacco output.

(c) Further privatization of sisal estates will increase output and carry out diversification of sisal products, such as use of sisal waste, geotextiles, etc. Privatization is needed to bring in capital and new technology.

(d) The improvement of roads particularly in smallholder tea areas, will contribute to a timely harvest and delivery of green leaf tea to factories and will therefore lead to an increase in the quantity and quality of made tea.

(e)   The market prospects for crude pyrethrum extract are dim but those for processed products are better. There is need to invest in processing facilities in order to maintain and even increase the profitability of pyrethrum.

Policy options

The types of interventions that are needed to complement economic reforms include: direct intervention to lower transport costs; adoption of policies that would increase productivity in the food sector; and improved marketing. Aggregate agricultural output can only increase in the long run if new resources move into the sector. This requires that non-price constraints are addressed by the government. What is needed is efficient government participation in agriculture along with the private sector. In general, the role of government should be to improve infrastructure, provide public goods, correct for externalities (effects caused during production that can be positive or negative, e.g., pollution), and directly increase the intensity of competition in the sector by its own presence.

Better efforts and approaches in dealing with the agricultural sector are required. The Ministry of Agriculture should be restructured to emphasize planning, monitoring, evaluation, rendering and coordinating agricultural research and extension services. After these institutional adjustments, strategies for increased sustained agricultural production must be put in place in order to enhance the role of the sector in:

(a)   increasing the output of food and export crops
(b)   processing agricultural crops for export and for the domestic market
(c)   developing off-farm activities with a view to raising employment and incomes in the rural areas in order to curb increasing rural-urban migration, and
(d)   enhancing the competence of the government in policy analysis and economic and development management, and putting in place regulatory mechanisms and institutional frameworks to ensure efficient functioning of the market.

Short-term policy options
In the short run, the first priority is to finalize plans for improved delivery of services. This includes the reorganization of the entire Ministry of Agriculture to emphasize planning, monitoring and coordination of activities

that will enhance output. In particular, plans to reorganize research and extension services must be completed and executed. The issue of better training and remuneration of extension and research staff is of paramount importance.

An efficient regulatory framework should be put in place to ensure that market reforms function well. This framework would include the collection and dissemination of information to farmers and traders; planning and evaluation; licensing of traders; grading of produce; and other regulatory activities needed for the smooth operation of markets.

Other short-term policy options include:

(a) liberalization of cross-border trade in food crops, which is particularly important for the southern food surplus regions

(b) the use of profitability and competitiveness to guide the production of export crops, and, on the other hand, the use of modern technology to enhance competitiveness, and

(c) greater expenditure by the government on services that can induce higher levels of income and productivity (such as extension and research).

Medium to long-term policy options
In general, greater efforts should be made to expand production in those areas of the country where there is still greater availability of high potential land, through the encouragement of the use of ox-ploughs, tractors and other farm implements. In particular, the following policy options should be considered:

(a) the revitalization of the export and food crop processing industries by allowing the private sector to invest on a competitive basis in processing facilities such as cotton ginning, cashew-processing and coffee hulling and curing

(b) the need to improve transportation and storage facilities at all levels of production and marketing in order to overcome bottlenecks which raise costs and endanger the competitiveness of Tanzania's exports, and to counter the negative effect of the poor state of transport infrastructure on agriculture

(c) the development of a system based on tenders which should be open to all participants instead of the agency system used in the Strategic Grain Reserve (SGR), and of a system of buying and releasing stocks, including ways of determining trigger prices at which the purchases/sales should be made

(d) the design and implementation of agricultural policies and extension services which encourage increased production of the non-traditional export crops such as horticulture, especially with smallholder farmers in mind, in order to diversify our exports, and

(e)   emphasis on irrigation based agricultural production and the development of a water resource management project to ensure the regulation of water use among many users and for various uses, e.g., agriculture and electricity generation.

The government should aid the development of rural credit facilities by encouraging informal, semi-informal and formal rural-based saving and credit societies. Donor and non-governmental agencies can work with the government on such innovative schemes that could pave the way for the development of private rural banks, and the cooperative movement can play a role in the development of such banks.

Tanzania's livestock sector needs to be developed. This should start with an inventory of the country's livestock resources and its characteristics, including production and marketing. Community-based improvement schemes can then be set up with the government helping in providing research, extension services and in designing packages that include credit facilities.

The government should also be in the forefront in checking the adverse environmental impact of agricultural growth to ensure sustained economic growth. The areas to watch out for in this regard are:

(a)   soil degradation, e.g., through the shortening of the fallow period due to land shortage

(b)   pollution of ground and surface water by agri-chemicals, and

(c)   encroachment on national parks, water sources, etc.

The regulatory function of government is needed to check the spread of these negative impacts. On the other hand, research and extension can lead to preventive and remedial measures in these areas.

Mining

Current status

Tanzania's main mineral development potential is in gold, diamonds and gemstones; energy minerals (coal, peat and uranium); iron ore and other base metals such as nickel, cobalt and the platinum group minerals; and a range of industrial minerals, including kaolin, soda ash, gypsum, mica, phosphate, salt and limestone. The performance of the mineral sector and its role in the national economy (especially during the 1970s and 1980s when the government was a major actor in mining activities through state enterprises) has been poor. In recognition of this, the government began to restructure the mineral sector from the late 1980s, albeit on a piecemeal basis. In particular, the introduction of macro-economic changes and mineral trade liberalization in 1990 had a positive impact on the mineral sector's contribution to the national economy.

In contrast to the declining trend in industrial mining, Tanzania has, since the early 1990s, seen a rapid and vigorous expansion of artisanal and small scale mining activities, concentrating on gold and gemstones. With the exception of diamonds, the production of these precious minerals has increased markedly as a result of the liberalized foreign exchange regime and the removal of government's restrictive mineral marketing policy. Substantial production has also been recorded for gypsum, limestone, salt and coal.

In 1993, the government started formulating a comprehensive Mineral Sector Policy Strategy Framework (MSPF) as well as an action plan to implement a series of reforms in legal, regulatory and fiscal regimes and institutional changes. The goal of the MSPF is to promote development of the mineral sector by the private sector. The role of the government is to provide the necessary enabling environment for private investment. Since the macro-economic restructuring process began, the role of the state has gradually changed from that of investor-operator of mineral ventures to that of administrator and promoter of the sector.

In order to speed up the implementation of the MSPF, in 1994 the government of Tanzania, with the assistance of the World Bank, formulated a Mineral Sector Development Technical Assistance Project with International Development Agency (IDA) financing. The primary objective of the project is to support Tanzania's policy of favouring the private sector approach to the development of mining and to expand private investment in mining. The secondary objective is to strengthen the capacity of the mineral sector institutions to efficiently administer and regulate the sector.

Consequent to the measures of macro-economic restructuring, coupled with trade liberalization, mining GDP grew by 46 percent between 1990 and 1992 and the value of mineral export earnings rose from US$16.75 million in 1989 to US$53.23 million in 1992. On average, mineral export earnings represent 8.5 percent of Tanzania's total export earnings. From 1993, there has been a substantial slump as the value of mineral export earnings has been declining. This slump has been occasioned by such factors as the inability of the financial institutions to offer a competitive market price for gold, lack of experience in the gold buying business, and mismanagement of the gold buying scheme by these financial institutions.

As a result of the failure of these institutions to meet the requirements of the market mechanism, the small-scale/artisanal producers of gold have often resorted to the parallel market. Consequently official gold purchases dropped from 4.5 tonnes recorded in 1992 to 2.86 tonnes in 1994, representing a 36.4 percent decrease.

There has been substantial interest in mineral exploration and development in the country since the beginning of the 1990s. Particular exploration interests have been in diamonds, gold, gemstones, base metals and industrial minerals. For example, in just three years (1992 to 1994) 256 active prospecting licences were issued to private local and foreign companies, compared to less than ten licences issued yearly before 1990. Also, between 1992 and 1994, eight specific mineral agreements were concluded between the government and foreign companies.

Problems and challenges

Although the government has recognized the importance of private investment and subsequently reduced or removed the requirement of the state's mandatory participation in mining ventures, the development of the sector is still beset by a number of negative factors. First is the lack of capital resources for mineral exploration and development, both of which require huge capital outlays. Due to a variety of reasons, mainly lack of significant private capital and non-involvement of financial institutions in financing mining activities, the requisite financial resources for these programmes have been difficult to generate internally. Second is Tanzania's inappropriate legislative and fiscal regime. Over the years, these regimes encouraged more state participation in the ownership of the mineral industry, which has been a deterrent to mineral resources development in Tanzania. The three elements of the investment climate, namely contractual relationship, taxation and political risk, have had the most bearing on mineral investment in Tanzania. The third negative factor, to which the failure of state-run mining enterprises has been attributed, is the lack of management skills, which are critical to resources development, combined with the non-emphasis on research and development (R&D) that has hindered technological innovation and renovation. Fourth is the global cyclical factor associated with periodic energy crises and global recessions, which have affected Tanzania's economic performance. Global competition for investment resources, which has influenced the restructuring of macro-economic policies world-wide, has, together with factors outlined above, made inevitable the need for private participation in the development of mineral resources and formulation of a Mineral Sector Policy.

Policy options

In order to address the developments and challenges that remain in the mineral sector the following policy options could be pursued.

Short-term policy options
The following should be given priority:

(a) finalization of the implementation arrangements of the Mineral Sector Policy for Tanzania which will define the government's role, objectives and strategies for encouraging and promoting exploration, development and utilization of the country's mineral resources
(b) organizational restructuring of the Mineral Resources Department in order to effectively administer, regulate and promote private investment in industrial mining ventures and foster the development of small-scale mining
(c) implementation of a priority work programme, which focuses on the (three) most urgent areas of mineral rights registration, mine safety and environmental inspection, and mineral revenue collection, and
(d) the establishment of investor confidence by reviewing the present complicated and deficient legal and fiscal structures to make mining legislation uniform, consistent, transparent and competitive.

The government must continue to improve policies aimed at providing an attractive enabling environment for investors in the mining sector. Specifically to this end, in 1992 the government announced its intention to revise the legal framework relating to mining to increase consistency and transparency, and to streamline licensing procedures.

Medium to long-term policy options
The government should consider the following policy options to enhance the performance of the mining sector in the medium to long-term.

(a) The development of the necessary manpower base and field experience, and provision of technical and managerial skills and operating systems is required to enable the Mineral Resources Department to carry out its functions more efficiently under the new mining legislation and regulations.
(b) The implementation of a small-scale mining programme aimed at promoting and controlling the sub-sector on a sustainable basis is needed. The objectives of such a programme are:
(i) to legalize the informal segment of the sub-sector and to

progressively transform it to formal small-scale mining operations

(ii)   to introduce a code of practice designed to improve health and safety standards and to largely eliminate undesirable environmental practices

(iii) to establish a reliable channel of supply of technologically appropriate mining and processing equipment, and

(iv)   to transform Regional Miners Associations into efficient and sustainable self-help organizations and training centres.

(c)   The establishment of industries that will provide direct services to the mineral sector should be encouraged and facilitated.

(d)   Environmental regulations and monitoring arrangements must be formulated.

(e)   The establishment of adequate institutional measures is necessary in order to position Tanzania at international level markets as a credible exporter of mineral commodities. To achieve this, the government ought to design effective marketing strategies and options that will discourage smuggling and illegal export of mineral products; and promote and encourage value added initiatives on mineral products and eliminate the present practice of sale of minerals at marginal value.

Industrial sector

Current status

The post-independence Tanzanian industrialization process began with a policy of import substitution, accompanied by rapid growth of the economy and the sector, raising the manufacturing contribution to the Gross Domestic Product from 4 percent in 1966 to about 12 percent in 1977. There then followed a period of de-industrialization during 1980 to 1984, when the economy recorded a marginal GDP growth of 0.8 percent per annum while the manufacturing sector declined at an annual average rate of 5 percent. A significant but temporary growth was recorded during 1985 to 1989 when the real GDP grew at 3.9 percent per annum and manufacturing grew at 2.3 percent. Official statistics indicate that the contribution of the industrial sector to the GDP declined from 10.2 percent between 1980 and 1984 to about 8 percent between 1990 and 1994.

Since the 1970s, the sector has shifted from what can be called basic primary export product processing (plus handicrafts) to increasingly domestic market-oriented supplying—providing the basic consumer goods and construction materials, with a small but growing intermediate and capital goods element based on metal working and light engineering. However, the structure of manufacturing output has remained unchanged within the food, beverage, tobacco, textiles and leather sub-sectors that were still dominant during the 1980s and 1990s. The contribution of these sub-sectors to total manufacturing value added (MVA) was, for example, around 48 percent in 1991 as compared to the chemicals sub-sector (24 percent), metals and engineering (13 percent), wood and allied products (nine percent), and non-metal sub-sectors (six percent). Only a few industries (tobacco, other chemicals and plastic) expanded to operate successfully while many others (textile and garments) continued to stagnate due to the various production constraints which have caused nearly all firms to perform below their capacities at installation.

In order to restructure the post-independence economy, the government formulated the Basic Industry Strategy (BIS) which was adopted in 1975. The industrial policy embodied in the BIS was basically intended to raise the degree of national economic integration by deepening vertical linkages between sectors and horizontal linkages across sectors. In this respect the enhancement of local value added goods was to be given priority through the exploitation of the local resources base for raw materials, and for the production of intermediate and capital goods in order to increasingly minimize the importation of basic final consumer goods.

At the same time, the manufacturing sector has been subjected to several trade and macro-economic policy measures in recent years (the 1980s and 1990s), such as structural adjustment and trade liberalization. The country has made major progress towards setting up a more favourable general policy environment for private sector expansion and growth. Most restrictive trade regulations and controls have been removed. Tanzania is moving from its previous reliance on control mechanisms toward a predominantly market-oriented environment. A major objective of the recent economic recovery programme has been to stimulate economic output by increasing producer incentives through improved terms of trade. However, it is widely accepted that the short and medium-term responses to the reform programmes have generally been poor. The manufacturing industry in particular has failed to expand output, employment, productivity and exports.

However, there are some positive elements in these reforms. Trade liberalization, which has introduced competition from imports and from domestic activities, has also led to an increased availability of a variety of quality and cheap consumer goods. It has introduced and facilitated the availability of raw materials and spare parts needed for production and rehabilitation of industries. Increased competition has induced efforts towards improvement of production efficiency and the quality of the final product. Economic liberalization has facilitated a switch from an inward to an outward-oriented trade policy as reflected in the comparative figures for the effective protection rates for 1984 and 1993, which show a substantial decrease in the rates for most activities. For example, between 1984 and 1993 the effective protection rate for food products fell from 532 percent to 35 percent; the rate for textiles and apparel fell from 335 percent to 24.67 percent; and the rate for beverages and tobacco fell from 240 percent to 39.19 percent.[5]

Basic supporting institutions
While creating the macro-economic environment necessary for sustained economic growth and development, the government has also put in place institutions to help promote growth in specific sectors. In the industrial sector, the government has legislated for the creation of the Investment Promotion Centre (IPC) through the Investment Promotion Act, 1990. The Act defined the functions of the IPC, and its powers in relation to the promotion, coordination and monitoring of foreign and local investment.

Investment Promotion Act and Centre
The main achievement of the Act is to simplify investment procedures by setting up the IPC as a one-stop shopping centre. Investments which are approved by the IPC qualify for still more generous fiscal incentives under the Investment Promotion Act, 1990, namely in the form of a five year tax holiday in which the investor pays no income tax whatsoever on his/her profits, and no withholding tax whatsoever on the dividends, interest and royalty payments. There is also full exemption from import duties and sales tax for all imports that are needed to establish the enterprises, including equipment, machinery, spare parts, raw materials and supplies.

Critiques have indicated that both the Act and IPC are outmoded and ineffective by performing what is mainly an essentially regulatory role— restricting entry of foreign investment or allowing it—rather than facilitating or promoting all kinds of investments, especially local ones. Indeed, the IPC seems to concentrate on small foreign investment activities that have a narrow impact on the achievement of its overall mandated objectives. There is a dire need to promote all investments, local as well as foreign, rather than to allow a few foreign investors to enjoy fiscal incentives. The IPC should operate as an independent private investment promotion institution with the challenge to promote private industrial development.

Technology supporting institutions and linkages
Between 1975 and 1995, as part of the Basic Industry Strategy, the government of Tanzania created a number of institutions whose purpose was to provide technological support to industry. These included the Tanzania Bureau of Standards (TBS) (1975), the Tanzania Industrial Studies and Consulting Organization (TISCO) (1976), the Tanzania Industrial Research

and Development Organization (TIRDO) (1979), the Institute for Production Innovation (IPI) (1979), the High Precision Technology Centre (HPTC) (1980), the Centre for Agricultural Mechanization and Rural Technology (CAMARTEC) (1981), and the Tanzania Engineering and Manufacturing Design Organization (TEMDO) (1983). This supporting institutional infrastructure was created to offer services to the industrial sector in their areas of competence to enable a sustainable growth within the sector.

Some of these public institutions are Research and Development (R&D) institutions (e.g., IPI, CAMARTEC, TEMDO and TIRDO). The major focuses of these R&D institutions are the design and manufacture of machinery and equipment for agriculture and of appropriate technologies for rural, medium and small-scale industrial enterprises. There are very few private industrial firms that are engaged in R&D activities in Tanzania. Low levels of R&D activities suggest that firms operate with short-term strategies and uncertainties of long-term investments.

The links that exist among industrial R&D institutions are weak. Where links do exist they are usually ad hoc in nature, normally driven by necessity and often dictated by the prevailing circumstances rather than technological strategy and deliberate planning. There is also a very weak link between R&D institutions and the private manufacturing sector, characterized by the failure to commercialize many R&D results and the failure to tackle the major technological problems facing productive activities in the economy. Many industrial firms also lack significant forward and backward linkages within the economy. This is due to the limited ability to locate efficient customers and input suppliers. Reliability of delivery is critical and sporadic and unreliable energy, transport and communications in the country undermine this. These problems are still serious impediments to technological capability and industrial development.

Outstanding problems

The lack of private indigenous investment remains a stumbling block to sustainable industrial development. The major weakness of the initial reforms is their almost exclusive focus on market efficiency. As a result, reforms have overlooked the need to offer selective protection for the many struggling indigenous industries. Recent studies suggest that reforms paid no attention to indigenous technological capacity building, and tended to favour trading rather than industrial manufacturing. The provision of incentives was also not transparent.

In industry, improvements have been made in relaxing foreign exchange allocation and in improved investment incentives. However, improvement in efficiency and capacity utilization has been slow and some sub-sectors have faced new constraints largely arising from the devaluation, financial reforms and import liberalization discussed in Chapter 1.

Many industries have had difficulties in adjusting to new competitive pressures as they had become used to operating under an import-substitution programme of industrialization which focused on supplying goods to a protected local market. Rapid deindustrialization within textile and garments is taking place due to the rampant untaxed and therefore cheap imports that do not offer fair competition to domestic products.

Local industries still face a number of serious constraints in just competing successfully in the domestic market, let alone in making the step to export. While most of the constraints encountered by local industry are related to import procedures rather than export procedures, they limit the number of new entrants into the export sector by restricting the growth of local industries. High production costs make it difficult for local industries to compete against cheap imports coming from countries in which industries have developed significant economies of scale. The poor infrastructure (i.e., poor roads leading into rural areas, lack of water for industrial use, and irregular electricity supply) is one of the primary causes of the high cost of production. The nation-wide dilemma caused by the current electricity fluctuations and shortages is forcing many companies to invest in thermo-equipment so as to be independent of the national grid supplies. At the macro-level, the energy problem has scared potential foreign investment, and intensified the existing problems related to capacity utilization and the settlement of the balance of payments. Digging bore holes, buying water, and running generators all add heavily to manufacturing costs at firm level.

Illegal imports undercut the ability of local industry to compete in domestic as well as export markets. Two of the main problems are the widespread practice of minimizing or avoiding duties by under-invoicing imported goods, particularly at the port of Zanzibar; and the practice of off-loading goods that have been declared for re-export to avoid paying sales tax. These practices affect manufacturers trying to export goods assembled from semi-finished components. Many goods are imported as raw materials, subject to lower tax rate, though they are really finished products and only require packaging. Local industry cannot compete with those prices, in domestic or export markets. No serious policy measures have been taken to reduce corruption at customs.

In general, the performance of the sector has not been very impressive for a number of reasons—high interest rates, accelerating inflation, the lack of adequate physical infrastructure and telecommunications, poor back up and maintenance facilities and business supporting constraints have all contributed. Many small and medium-sized industries have had a limited capacity to invest in technology and modernization of their aging plant and machinery partly because of their weakened financial position.

The design of economic reforms has not paid adequate attention to the low level of markets, institutions and capabilities. It has ignored comparative advantage by not giving a chance to potentially competitive activities to develop. The policies and institutions that have been put in place have not adequately facilitated the process of technological upgrading.

Industrial development is influenced by how well firms manage the complex process of technological development, a process that faces various market failures. In this context, protection is necessary to induce entry into activities with relatively difficult learning processes but this protection must be limited in extent and duration, preferably combining domestic protection of industry with strong export-orientation. This is justified because learning costs differ between activities, in which case intervention will need to be selective rather than uniform.

Lessons from newly industrialized economies (NIEs) that could be relevant to Tanzania suggest that a variety of state interventions, active industrial policies and sound macro-economic management facilitated their industrialization process. Domestic resources were channelled to selected infant industries with the encouragement to export as they approached competitiveness. The state provided a wide range of technology supportive services. The various models that emerged in the NIEs were differentiated by the strategy to tackle market failures but common to all of them is the adoption of interventions to protect the learning process and to facilitate industrial deepening in the context of a strongly export-oriented trade regime. Foreign investment was used to feed local technological effort and not to replace it.

Possible solutions

In industrialization, broad-based growth implies higher growth of industry while improving employment generating effects, trade performance and competitiveness. In the past, economic efficiency and technological dynamism have been relatively neglected goals of industrial policy. There were few incentives to reduce cost and improve quality. Industrial policy should be tailored to developing efficient import substitution and dynamic manufactured exports.

The future of industrial development in Tanzania is likely to be influenced by four main considerations. First, the balance of agents of industrial development and investors in the sector will shift in favour of the private sector. Second, the role of market forces is likely to be enhanced at the expense of administrative controls. Third, greater weight will need to be placed on considerations of regional and international competitiveness.

Lastly, there is an imperative need to develop a strategic domestic industrial base as a foundation for medium-term objectives of socio-economic transformation towards self-sustaining economic growth and development.

There are suggestions that the country has the potential to increase its industrial output and share of industry by 4 percent to 5 percent during the next three years through increased efficiency and improved capacity utilization within existing industries, and through the development of new industries in the key sub-sectors of the small and medium scale industrial sector. Low capacity utilization, a weak financial supporting system and low production technologies may continue to limit the growth of large scale manufacturing firms. Therefore, there is an urgent need to promote small scale and medium scale industries for the purpose of increasing industrial output, generating employment, developing sector linkages and ensuring rural industrial development.

Strategies to be used to effect this broad-based development plan include the improvement of access to credit and foreign exchange and the development of new forms of credit institutions such as venture capital and stock markets. Tanzania has continued to put in place an incentive framework (e.g., the Investment Code of 1990) for domestic and foreign investment. A series of measures could be introduced to bring about considerable economic benefits. These measures include: easing forex constraints; reducing restrictions on borrowing of foreign companies; broad-ownership privatization policies; opening up more areas of the manufacturing sector to private investors; and reorganizing the present business and technological institutions.

Access to financing by business firms should be improved, especially in the case of those companies which are African owned, involve new entrants or are small firms. In future, the availability of credit may be relatively easier for entrepreneurs who have collateralizable assets, but there is no obvious reason to believe that the owner's wealth and the growth potential of the firm would be correlated.

The most dangerous weakness of the infrastructure is frequent power shortages. It would be most advisable to channel investments into the power production and distribution network. Roads and telephones are problematic as well, and these deficiencies are likely to lead to an unexpected reallocation of resources. Other growth based measures include: easing regulatory obstacles such as cumbersome licensing procedures; provision of adequate zoning laws and ascertaining land tenure; providing adequate infrastructural support services such as water and feeder roads; encouraging subcontracting between small and large scale enterprises; promoting small scale industries in government procurement schemes; and using relatively efficient production technologies.

Economic services sectors are instrumental in contributing to development directly or indirectly by facilitating the development of other sectors. This chapter addresses the current status, challenges and policy options in transport, telecommunications, energy, water and sanitation, and tourism.

Transport

Current status

The transport sector plays a critical role as a lubricant, stimulator and facilitator of economic, social and political development. Any modern economy would simply grind to a halt without transport, as would an engine without lubrication. The pattern of settlement and economic activity gives transportation an extraordinarily strategic role in economic development.

The contribution of the transport sector to the GDP has been growing in Tanzania. While the GDP grew at an average rate of 3.7 percent between 1990 and early 1994, the transport sector grew at an average rate of almost 8 percent during the same period. This remarkable contribution is a result of the emphasis placed on the reconstruction and rehabilitation of major transport infrastructures aimed at providing effective services to other sectors of the economy.

The transport system in Tanzania comprises five sub-sectors, namely:

(a)   a road network of about 88,000 kms
(b)   two railway systems totalling about 3,510 kms of track within Tanzania operated by Tanzania Railway Corporation (TRC) (2600 kms) and by Tanzania Zambia Railway Authority (TAZARA) (970 kms)
(c)   ocean ports managed and operated by Tanzania Harbours Authority (THA)
(d)   three international airports and numerous other smaller aerodromes and air strips, and
(e)   a pipeline which conveys crude oil products from Dar es Salaam to Zambia.

The road transport sub-sector plays a major role in the movement of goods and passengers. Over 70 percent of freight transport is estimated to be by road. The total road network covers about 88,000 kms. Of this, 10,300 kms are primary (trunk) roads, 17,730 kms are secondary (regional) roads, 30,000 kms are feeder and district/urban roads and 30,000 kms are unclassified roads.

The road network had deteriorated to such a bad state that by 1990 only about 15 percent of the trunk road network and only 10 percent of rural roads (including regional roads) were in good condition. Since then high priority has been given to road rehabilitation and maintenance. By 1993/94 over 40 percent of the government development budget was allocated to infrastructure, of which the largest share went to the transport sector, especially roads. The Roads Fund, financed from a road user charge collected mainly from fuel, has been put in place. The Fund is for financing the maintenance of roads.

As a result of reforms that have been effected in the road maintenance administration system, and also considering the road rehabilitation, upgrading and backlog periodic maintenance works that have been carried out over the last four years, very substantial progress has been made. For example, the proportion of trunk roads in good condition has more than doubled while that of regional and selected rural roads has increased by almost 40 percent. Yet there is still a lot to be done. A survey conducted by the Ministry of Works, Communication and Transport (MWCT) in 1994 found that 40 percent of trunk roads were in good condition, 39 percent in fair condition, and 21 percent in poor condition. The figures for regional roads were 18 percent in good condition, 43 percent in fair condition, and 39 percent in poor condition.

Today the private sector dominates the road transport operations subsector in Tanzania. Private sector participation in road freight and passenger transportation stands at 80 percent to 90 percent. The majority of operators are small fleet owners who own an average of from one to three trucks with carrying capacity of between one tonne and 15 tonnes.

A large proportion of these private operators prefers to operate on inter-regional routes. The attractive business opportunities and lower operational costs as compared to intra-regional routes, which are characterized by more rugged infrastructure conditions and short hauls, can explain this.

The public sector has also been involved in road transport operations. The operations are of two main categories, the first one comprising companies whose core business is transportation, such as Regional Transport Companies (RETCOs) and Usafiri Dar es Salaam (UDA). The second category are those institutions in which transport is only a supportive facility to their core business activities, for example, Tanzania Breweries, crop marketing boards, Cooperative Unions, etc.

Progress continues to be made in improving the management, financing, rehabilitation and maintenance of infrastructure, particularly in the area of road transport. Much of this progress is due to the completion of the first phase of the multi-donor-financed Integrated Roads Projects (IRP). The second phase of IRP is now being implemented.

The TRC and TAZARA railway lines link Tanzania to six of her seven neighbouring countries, four of which are land locked. Because the TRC system has a narrower gauge, similar to that in Kenya and Uganda, it has not been possible to link it up with the central and southern African railways systems. TRC's railway network is made up of 2,605 kms of one metre gauge. Of this, the Dar es Salaam to Kigoma section is 1,252 kms, the Dar es Salaam to Mwanza route is 1,229 kms and the Dar es Salaam to Arusha route is 625 kms. Tanga port is linked to the railway system by a line to Mnyusi near Korogwe. The TRC system is linked to similar railway systems in Kenya and Uganda through wagon ferries operating on Lake Victoria. The inland waterways system on Lake Tanganyika links the TRC system network to Eastern Zaire and Burundi. TRC is also linked to the Kenya railways system through the Kahe-Taveta branch line in the north of the country, while in the south the system is in very close proximity to the wider 1.067 metre gauge TAZARA at Dar es Salaam and Kidatu. The TAZARA links 10 Southern Africa Development Community (SADC) countries, plus Zaire, with several lines of the same gauge, making a total network of about 30,000 kms of main lines. The railway also links the 10 countries to 11 ports including Dar es Salaam.

Through the Directorate of Civil Aviation (DCA), the government operates an elaborate system of air routes backed up by a variety of navigation and communication systems installed at airports and within the Flight Information Region (FIR) to ensure safe, orderly and efficient flow of air traffic in Tanzanian airspace. There are three international airports (Dar es Salaam, Kilimanjaro and Zanzibar); six major domestic airports; 54 other airports and air fields, and 73 air strips.

Regarding air operations, there were about 200 aircraft registered in Tanzania by May 1994. However, a significant increase in the number of registered aircraft was noted immediately after the introduction of a liberalized air services licensing policy in 1992 and the removal of Air Tanzania Corporation (ATC)'s monopoly of the provision of scheduled air services. By 1995, over 33 air operators had been licensed by the Civil Aviation Board (CAB) compared to only eight previously. Out of the licensed air operators, six are licensed to operate scheduled air services. Unfortunately, most of the newly licensed operators have proved to be ineffective and thus have failed to take off because of their failure to meet air operations certificate requirements. In fact, domestic air transport operations have been decreasing, mainly due to a number of reasons. These include:

(a) ATC's closure of routes which are considered to be uneconomic, because of its limited capacity
(b) limited or poor airport facilities that have reduced the frequency of flights to some airports (e.g., lack of lighting and other navigational

facilities, useful for night landing/ take off), and
(c)   the availability of alternative cheaper modes of transport such as roads (especially after the improvements made on the roads, which have encouraged investment in highway passenger transport and reduced travel time by a big margin compared to the time prior to rehabilitation).

Regarding the international air services, there are 16 foreign air lines which combine to operate almost 40 weekly flights at Dar es Salaam International Airport (DIA), Kilimanjaro International Airport (KIA) and Zanzibar. Generally, the contribution of Tanzania to international air transport services is minimal.

The Dar es Salaam port consists of three container berths (Nos. 9-11); eight general cargo berths (Nos. 1-8); an oil products terminal; wharfs for coastal and passenger traffic; and a dockyard. All of these facilities are located on the western shore of the inner harbour. In addition to facilities on the waterfront, the port also operates two inland container depots (at Ubungo and Kurasini).

Dar es Salaam port has more facilities and more capacity than all the other ports in the country combined. The Tanga port, which is second in size, consists of two lighterage dhow wharfs with a total of 581 meters, nine stream handling points and nine lighterage area transit sheds. The port of Mtwara is the third in size and has a lot fewer facilities.

For shipping operations, Tanzania is blessed with a long coastline and several inland waterways that link it with neighbouring countries. Despite this situation there does not appear to be any effective system or strategy to enable the country to fully exploit this important transport resource. For instance, Tanzania has minimal participation in deep-sea shipping, and in addition has not yet developed water transport systems on its major rivers such as the Rufiji and the Ruvuma. However, motorized and non-motorized small boats are in use in some areas (including the coastline) for fishing and transport activities, and the TRC Marine Department is providing regular marine services in the three main lakes, which are Victoria, Tanganyika and Nyasa.

Currently there is continued emphasis on maintenance and rehabilitation of the transport infrastructure, while selected new investments are undertaken. The second phase of the Integrated Roads Programme (implemented from 1994/95) is focusing on strengthening the transport sector administration, particularly through the separation of policy making and regulatory functions from management of operations; improving commercial operations of road transport parastatals; the strengthening of organizational, management and financing arrangements for the road network, including ensuring road charges remain at levels necessary to fully fund all maintenance costs (with the exception of periodic backlogs of maintenance); and the rehabilitation and upgrading of the trunk, regional, and rural road networks.

Outstanding problems and challenges

Presently, accessibility to most rural areas is still a big problem. Rural areas are still constrained by poor infrastructure and lack of transport services. The accessibility of most villages is seasonal. Since most of the rural dwellers are poor, they usually cannot afford motorized forms of transport. The bulk of the investment being made under the IRP I and II for roads (US$1.5 billion altogether) concentrates on the existing trunk and regional roads and a few selected district roads. However, awaiting the further development of local government, little attention is being paid to the secondary and feeder road system that provides access for the rural communities to the other localities in the district and further on to the regional and trunk roads.

There are many parts of the country with high potential for development, such as areas with iron and coal deposits, tourist attractions and good agricultural land. Some or most of these areas are either not accessible by trunk roads or the existing roads are in such poor shape that they limit the exploitation of these potentials.

In fast growing urban centres, particularly the city of Dar es Salaam, private public service vehicles (daladalas)[6] continue to dominate the scene and the envisaged sustainable urban transport companies are yet to emerge despite the liberalization of the transport industry. The quality of service in terms of conventional means of transport is also yet to be achieved since a significant proportion of privately owned vehicles are converted trucks whose safety and comfort are obviously unsatisfactory. Furthermore, the state of traffic management in urban areas and especially within Dar es Salaam is critical. This situation compounds the problem of congestion and the resultant pollution, noise and road accidents. UDA continues to operate at a loss, and there is a lack of more organized institutions or companies providing transport services in the major urban areas. This presents another hurdle to the enhamcement of efficient transport services.

The main problems that are being encountered in air transport include lack of appropriate communication, navigation and fire fighting equipment, poor runways, airport buildings, navigational aid facilities, etc. The fundamental problem is that airports are managed as part of government departments without managerial autonomy or clearly defined financial objectives. This problem needs rectifying.

Coordination of the railways and ports operations and other agencies is another challenge. Being a sum total of the functions rendered by all operators en route, total competence depends on handling efficiency at the ports; the speed at which customs handle and clear documents; reduced red tape by immigration; efficient clearing and forwarding agencies; and efficiency and capacity of transport modes such as railways and road haulers, etc. The total sum of the costs, time and efficiency, and safety of the route would determine the competitiveness and acceptability of that route.

The end of apartheid in South Africa and the achievement of peace in Mozambique and Angola have not only opened up other transit routes for Southern Africa but have also put an end to the privileged or monopolistic position that Tanzania enjoyed in its transit route. Now Tanzania faces stiff competition. Effort is required to ensure that Tanzania continues to provide a competitive route for landlocked countries.

Financing of transport infrastructure and operations is a major problem in the development of the transport sector. Most of the on-going development programmes such as the IRP for the roads, the Railway Restructuring Programme for TRC, the Ten Year Development Plan for TAZARA and Port Modernization Programme are all dependent on donor funding. This is risky, considering growing donor fatigue. There is need to rethink the traditional funding approach which leans heavily on a government budget that supplements donor funds. The involvement of private sector resources in sector development is an issue that needs to be stressed. There is also a need to reconsider the tradition of depending on donor initiatives and funds even for minor maintenance and rehabilitation of economic infrastructures. Grassroot initiatives that were common during the 1960s are no longer operational because the supposition is that the government will do everything.

Some transport facilities and services are still being provided and managed directly by the government through various departments, which, however, are subjected to civil service bureaucracy, budgeting needs and procedures. The majority of these services could easily be divested and operated and managed by either autonomous agencies or by the private sector on a commercial basis. This would free the government to deal purely with its core functions such as law and order. Regarding essential services provided by parastatals, it is necessary to streamline their operations to ensure efficiency.

Policy options

The government must consider the following requirements in order to improve the transport and communications sector.

(a) There is a need to strengthen the government's capacity to administer policy formulation, supervision, coordination, regulation and monitoring functions to create an environment for fair competition by operators.

(b) It is necessary to separate operating functions from the direct control of the government and ensure that parastatals function as commercial and autonomous entities.

(c) There is also a need for the government to commit itself to a continuous process of rational prioritization and monitoring of public sector expenditures, and of the formulation and consistent application of economic criteria in ranking all transport expenditures before major investment decisions are taken. Furthermore, the government should pursue optimum use of domestic resources and labour-based technologies and try to build environmental protection aspects into planning and implementation. In addition, it needs to recognize the need for increased use of information technology to ensure improved data collection and analysis, as well as effective execution of the Transport Ministry's functions of supervision, coordination, monitoring and regulation of the transport sector. In order to achieve this end, well-focused training will have to be given to all relevant personnel and a synchronized acquisition of information technology hardware and software will have to be carried out on a continuous basis.

(d) In the railways sub-sector the operators (i.e., TRC and TAZARA) will have to be allowed to continue to operate on a commercial basis without much interference from the government.

(e) In the ports sub-sector, the government will have to continue the process of decentralizing responsibility for operating functions away from headquarters to the ports. As for the maritime and shipping business, the challenge for the government is to speed up the reviewing of the relevant legislation related to institutions such as the National Shipping Agencies Corporation (NASACO), Tanzania Central Freight Bureau (TCFB), etc., with a view to streamlining and levelling the playing field for all operators in the industry.

(f) In the air transport sub-sector the government needs to restructure the Directorate of Civil Aviation and to create a national airports agency to manage, operate and maintain major airports. Other airports could continue to be managed by central or local government or by the airports agency, but also enjoy government subsidy. As for airlines, the "open skies" policy should be encouraged for improvement in competition and efficiency, and hence in the product supply.

(g) Overall, there is a need to instill and emphasize the culture of "maintenance rather than rehabilitation" from the grassroots to the national level. As part of a national self-reliance policy, people-centred initiatives such as those of rural road maintenance on a voluntary basis should thus be encouraged and given the necessary government support. Dependence on donor financing should be replaced with domestic financing.

Telecommunications

Current status

The efficient transport of goods and services requires the efficient communication of information. This is the function of the tele-communications sector. The most recent institutional change that took place in Tanzania in 1993 was the separation of operational from regulatory functions. The government split Tanzania Posts and Telecommunications Corporation (TPTC) into two separate operational enterprises—one to run telecommunications activities and the other to run postal services. The Tanzania Telecommunication Company (TTCL) took over the running of telecommunications activities. In addition, the government set up the Tanzania Telecommunication Commission to carry out regulatory functions in the telecommunications sector—issuing licences regulating technical matters related to telecommunications such as equipment, specifications, standards, etc.

TTCL has a monopoly of certain telecommunication services such as telephones. However, some ancillary services, such as mobile telephone services, have been opened to private enterprise.

Issues and challenges

TTCL has 87,300 direct exchange lines (DELs) which means there are 0.3 telephone lines per one hundred people. This is an extremely low telephone density, even by sub-Saharan standards. Meanwhile, the number of people waiting to be connected has increased from 60,000 ten years ago to about 145,000. This does not take into account people who have been discouraged from applying by either the long waiting period and/or by observing that even those connected have their telephones more or less permanently out of order.

Given TTCL's inability to finance future expansion, the waiting list will grow longer. Furthermore, telecommunications is a new technology intensive. TTCL lacks the experience, the capital and knowledge to acquire this technology. This points to the need for the entry of private participants into the main telecommunications business to increase its effectiveness.

The other issue is how to extend telephones and other services to the rural areas given TTCL's present inability to supply the service and its limitations in capital, technology and managerial capability. For rural telecommunications, there is need for a study of the kind of technology required for simple telecommunications and not necessarily installing private telephones in people's homes.

Policy options

The following options can be taken singly or in combination.

(a) Commercialization of TTCL needs careful consideration. TTCL must, through a performance contract, be forced to improve its operational and financial performance in order to quicken the pace at which it installs new lines and the efficiency with which it maintains existing lines.

(b) More capital and modern technology should be gained so that TTCL can:
(i)   enter into management contracts to run some of the services (in some regions)
(ii) enter into joint ventures with external partners
(iii) lease some of its facilities to others on a contractual basis, and/or
(iv) invite Tanzania Electric Supply Company (TANESCO), TRC TAZARA to provide some of the services in some parts of the country using their network.

(c) TTCL could be privatized completely.

Energy issues

Current status

Current energy balance
In order to facilitate the desired national broad-based economic growth, the articulation of a transitional energy development policy option is important. Tanzania's energy demand and end-use pattern is characteristic of that observed in other net-oil importing developing countries. More than 90 percent of the population depend on firewood as a source of fuel. This amounts to 90 percent of the country's total energy consumption. The total demand for wood fuel stands at about 43 million cubic metres per year. Wood fuel is used mainly for domestic cooking, and for industrial processes such as tobacco curing, tea processing, fish smoking, pottery, baking and brewing.

Wood fuel and other forms of biomass constitute about 92.2 percent of the energy balance. Commercial energy sources are mainly petroleum and electricity, which account for 9.8 percent and 2.4 percent of energy supply respectively. Although the country is dependent on imports of fuel, there is potential to substitute these with domestic sources such as coal, natural gas, hydro-power, and solar, wind and biomass power. Oil, hydro-electricity and fuel wood are the three main forms of primary energy used in Tanzania. In 1993 petroleum products accounted for 74 percent, electricity for 24.3 percent and gas accounted for only 1.7 percent of the total commercial energy production.

Energy performance and problems
The performance of the energy sector was unsatisfactory during 1991/92 and 1994/95 due to frequent breakdowns at the generating plants, and lack of spare parts and foreign exchange, as well as the fall in the water level at Mtera Dam due to a long period of drought. This necessitated load shedding.

The rationing of power had a serious negative impact on the productive sectors. The GDP contribution of energy and water supply sectors dropped by 2.9 percent in 1994. Overdependence on biomass fuel can lead to negative effects on the environment such as soil erosion, changes in the weather, etc.

To mitigate the problems of power shortages, thermal generation had to be stepped up, increasing the country's fuel importation bill. Inadequate or nonexistent funding coupled with the depreciation of the local currency caused delays in the implementation of development projects.

Energy growth potential
Electricity
While Tanzania's energy resources are substantial and diverse, they have remained relatively unexploited. The country is fortunate in having a number of potential hydro-power sites that can satisfy its power requirements for many years. The total hydro-power potential has been estimated at about 4,500 MW, with about 20,000 GWh output per year. Of this potential, only 330 MW have been developed. The major sites with hydro-electric potential are found in the Rufiji River Basin and by far the largest single hydro-power potential site there is at Stiegler's Gorge. Tanzania has a large number of other potential sites, particularly in the western and southern parts of the country. Most of the potential involves schemes of more than two MW capacity, but some 1,000 Gwh/year are believed to rely on plants with an isolated capacity of less than two MW, which can be mini hydro-power sites. These can be developed for the production of electricity on a small scale to serve the needs of remote and isolated areas.

At present the electricity supply system operated by TANESCO consists of an interconnected grid serving the major towns, and a number of isolated grids serving areas located away from the main grid. The installed power capacity in Tanzania is 485.9 MW in 1992, of which 70 percent comes from hydro-power and the rest from thermal power plants. The isolated grids are scattered throughout the country and have an installed capacity of around 28 MW of diesel generated power. There is another grid consisting of 6 MW at Cairo coal fired power plant near Tukuyu operated by the State Mining Corporation (STAMICO). There are also a large number of small private power generators, registered at the Ministry of Water, Energy and Minerals. Although TANESCO's power generation capacity additions are planned ahead of time, the record of implementation has been marred by limited ability to finance the planned installations. For instance, the Pangani Falls Redevelopment (690 MW) which was planned for 1992 and Lower Kihansi (162 MW) which was planned for 1994 were both delayed owing to lack of finance.

The TANESCO system energy losses are very high, averaging around 25 percent of the energy generated. These losses have resulted from theft, aging and underrated equipment, erroneous meter reading, transformer overload, excessive reliance on low voltage lines, poor maintenance and use of inappropriate materials. It is crucial to develop strategies to reduce transmission and distribution losses to an acceptable range of 5 to10 percent.

Mini hydro-power units are viewed as locally available and affordable energy sources that can contribute to the stimulation of economic activities and the raising of rural living standards. There are a significant number of mini hydro units, and most of them are in the Iringa region. This region is one of the most suitable areas for mini hydro-power since it has many rivers and waterfalls. It is estimated that there are more than 75 mini hydro-power potential sites of up to two MW of installed capacity. Their total installed capacity is about 35 MW. The distribution of mini-hydro resources is such that 77 percent of the sites have a capacity of less than one MW and 23 percent have a capacity of one to two MW. Lack of engineering information in the rural areas, low expected economic returns, lack of mini hydro-power investment funds and lack of proper rural energy policy are the major factors limiting the development of mini hydro-power.

Coal and natural gas reserves
Coal has entered the energy scene very recently. It is presently used for power generation for a township (6 MW), in a cement factory and in a pulp and paper mill. In the southwestern area of the country, coal reserves have been estimated at 1.6 billion tonnes, of which 304 million tonnes are considered proven. The production in 1994 was 11,000 tonnes.

At the end of 1990, the proven recoverable reserves of natural gas were about 24 billion cubic metres. The reserves are located on Songo Songo Island and Mnazi Bay north of the Mozambique border.

Biomass resources
Tanzania has considerable biomass resources in terms of forestry and agricultural residues. The total forested area is 44 million hectares, about 50 percent of the total land area. To a varying extent, possibilities exist for an economic conversion of these resources to energy purposes. The current quantity of forest and crop residues is estimated at 1.1 million tonnes and 15 million tonnes respectively per annum and could account for at least 10 percent of the nation's energy requirements. However, this forest resource is harvested at a faster rate than it is replenished. Due to the increase in arid and semi-arid areas and in forest degradation, firewood is not considered to be a renewable energy source. The most effective measure towards helping the acute shortage of energy in villages is probably the introduction of more efficient cooking stoves for better utilization of the wood fuel available.

Challenges and outstanding issues

TANESCO's inability to utilize its power generation capacity more effectively to provide its customers with a satisfactory level of service is attributable, directly or indirectly, to government actions or inaction. As the power sector regulating authority, the government or the Ministry responsible for energy must approve increases in electricity tariffs greater than 10 percent per annum. As the single largest electricity customer, the government's payment obligations to TANESCO, together with those of its parastatals, account for more than one tenth of TANESCO's sales. Furthermore, the government's own development policies require that it not only mobilize financing in the form of loans and grants for major investments in the power sector, but it must also co-finance rural electrification projects in order to stimulate rural development without making TANESCO bankrupt or raising electricity tariffs beyond affordable levels. Finally, as TANESCO's sole shareholder the government is the appointing authority for its Board of Directors as well as its chief executive officer and is, as such, ultimately responsible for the efficiency or otherwise of TANESCO's operations. The problems associated with the government's role in the areas of electricity pricing, payment of electricity bills, financing of development projects and management of TANESCO are discussed below.

Until the mid 1980s electricity tariffs were generally in line with power supply costs. However, following the sharp and steady devaluation of the

Tanzania shilling which began in 1986, tariff revisions have not kept pace with the long run marginal cost of supply. This is due to the fact that over 90 percent of the cost of electricity is actually incurred in foreign currency for investment in generation, transmission and distribution facilities and their maintenance. Electricity tariffs have, on average, remained below the long run marginal cost of supply, which has been estimated to be equivalent to approximately US$.09 per kWh.In 1985 the average tariff paid by electricity consumers was just over US$ 0.11 cents per kWh. By 1990 this had dropped to about US$ 0.05, well below the long run marginal cost of supply. By 1993 the average tariff had increased to a little under US$ 0.07, prompted in part by the serious financial problems that TANESCO was then experiencing. These low tariff levels mean that not enough revenue has been generated by TANESCO from the sale of electricity to reliably meet growing demand.

For political reasons, the government has been reluctant to allow electricity tariffs to be periodically revised upward so as to stay above the cost of power supply. Although TANESCO may revise tariffs semi-annually by up to five percent without the government's approval, this amount has not been adequate to keep pace with the devaluation of the Tanzania Shilling. In addition, since 1992 the cost of supplying power has increased above the estimated long run marginal cost, mainly because of the need to use large amounts of liquid fuel to generate electricity in the short to medium-term to compensate for hydro-power insufficiency.

Industrial and commercial consumers account for the largest share of electricity sales, although the trend has been for residential consumers to account for an increasing share, partly because power tariffs in this sector are subsidized by the industrial consumers. In 1985 the average tariff for residential consumers was less than half that for industrial consumers. By 1990 residential consumers were being charged just 16 percent to 18 percent of the tariff paid by industries, and in 1993 they paid, on average, one third of what industries paid for their electricity. Not surprisingly, during the period from 1985 to 1990, before the onset of severe power rationing, the average power consumption of residential customers nearly doubled, while that of industrial customers increased by less than 20 percent. In 1993 industry and commerce accounted for 52 percent of sales. The residential sector accounted for 36 percent and other sectors for 12 percent.

The long-outstanding debts that the government and its parastatals owe TANESCO have typically been over Tshs.10 billion since 1993. TANESCO's accounts receivables grew from about seven months' sales in 1990 to nearly eight months' sales in 1993, while two months is the industry norm for efficiency. TANESCO has made a concerted effort to reduce its receivables by disconnecting large, delinquent customers, but this effort has often been hindered in the case of government or major parastatal customers by political intervention. The Ministry of Finance has been unable to fully honour the government's 1993 commitment, made in a power sector development credit agreement with the World Bank, to pay directly to TANESCO electricity bills for institutions that the government does not allow to be disconnected. TANESCO has had to resort to meeting its operational funding needs and even ongoing capital investment needs using a bank overdraft facility. This has further undermined its financial position because of the facility's high cost.

The government has traditionally received bilateral and multilateral funding as grants or on concessionary terms for development projects, including rural electrification projects, and has also been contributing local funds from its development budget for such projects. Since 1990 funding agencies' interest in financing rural electrification and public power utilities has declined. They have endorsed a new global trend towards the promotion of private investment in the power sector. As a result the pace of rural electrification in particular has slowed down. The government's ability even to maintain its funding of rural electrification projects at past levels in the short to medium-term is doubtful. As of December 1995 no funds have been made available for rural electrification from the government's 1995/96 development budget. This lack of funds imposes standby costs on TANESCO for ongoing projects, or forces it to use its scarce internal resources to continue with their implementation.

TANESCO has some internal weaknesses adding to the above financial difficulties that cannot be directly traced to the government. These are most evident in TANESCO's billing, accounting and financial management functions, as well as in the level of staff productivity and quality of customer service.TANESCO's billing and accounting systems are outmoded and unable to cope with the present demand for electricity services. Because meter-reading by TANESCO staff is frequently unreliable and all bills are prepared in Dar es Salaam, there is a delay of up to four months before customers are billed, with the amounts involved increasingly disputed. The preparation of audited annual accounts is currently at least 18 months behind the statutory deadline, reducing the ability of TANESCO's management and Board of Directors to monitor and manage its activities effectively. It also undermines staff accountability, particularly in the regional branches. With only about 30 customers per employee, TANESCO's labour productivity is low even by African standards.

Policy options

The major objectives of the energy sector are to satisfy the energy demand of all sectors of the economy, particularly the productive sectors, and to develop domestic sources of energy to substitute for imported petroleum products. Improvement of the availability, reliability and security of energy supply requires the rehabilitation of existing energy systems, including generators, transmission and storage facilities, and the expansion of power generation and distribution capacity. The national energy policy aims to supply reliable power to the majority of the people and at an affordable cost. Specific objectives of this transitional policy can be summarized as:

(a) exploitation of the abundant hydro-electric sources
(b) development and utilization of indigenous natural gas and coal resources
(c) escalation of petroleum exploration activities
(d) reduction in the pace of wood fuel depletion through the evolution of more appropriate land management practices and more efficient wood technologies
(e) provision for the continuity and security of energy supplies
(f) minimization of energy price fluctuations in order to contribute to general price stability, through strengthening and rationalization of energy supply sources, infrastructure provision, and maintenance of a rational energy pricing structure, and
(g) investment in appropriate human resources for energy sector management and energy technology development.

To establish an efficient energy production, procurement, transportation, distribution and end-use system in an environmentally sound manner, the government strategy aims to achieve the above objectives in collaboration with the private sector.

The government is undertaking a comprehensive review of the power sector to determine if all or parts of it should be and can be privatized. It will also continue the process of streamlining TANESCO and putting it on a viable commercial footing. The government has already brought average tariff rates in line with the long run marginal cost.

Water and sanitation

Current status

Water is a natural resource that plays an important role in economic activities. Availability of water does not only impact on the health and sanitation of human communities; it also impacts on their development by influencing the level and progress of productive economic activities in the urban and rural areas. The centrality of water in human life demands the proper articulation of policies to guide the development of water supply and serve its efficient utilization. In this regard, the long-term objective of the government is to make water available to within 400 yards of all rural and urban communities by 2002.

By 1994, a water supply had been made available to about 46 percent of the rural and 68.5 percent of the urban population. Nonetheless, the water sub-sector is confronted with a diverse set of problems. The inadequacies in the water sub-sector have hit the densely populated areas most severely, especially the urban areas. The infrastructure for urban water supplies developed during the colonial period is old. The amount of resources channelled to this sector has been inadequate to meet the increase in demand caused by an increase in the speed of urbanization. For example, while the 1990 water requirement in the urban areas was estimated at 229.7 million gallons per day (mgd), the supply of water was estimated at 122.124 mgd— about 53 percent of the water requirements.

Development of water supply infrastructure has also become impaired by a number of factors. The first factor is the lack of systematic assessment of the long-term water demand pattern, which has caused development investment policies in the sector to be based on ad hoc assessments. The second factor is the monopoly bestowed on the National Urban Water Authority (NUWA). This parastatal was established by an Act of Parliament in 1981 to supply water in the urban areas. As in most other parastatals, the services served by the NUWA remained inadequate in quality and coverage. In effect, the development and supply of water by the NUWA has been limited to Dar es Salaam, thus excluding other major urban centres, particularly Dodoma, Mwanza, Arusha and Tanga. The third factor is the lack of finance for new investment, operations and maintenance. The operational and maintenance funds allocated by the government to NUWA and to the regional water departments have been inadequate to meet the actual costs. Furthermore, the ability of the NUWA and the regional water authorities to set water prices remains handcuffed by the Ministry of Water, Energy and Minerals which possesses the authority for tariff reviews. Financial bottlenecks of the NUWA and other urban water authorities can be explained by an extreme inability to collect revenue coupled with the diversion of funds to other uses outside the water supply sector. The fourth factor is poor pricing policy. The tariff is too low, meaning that the NUWA loses money, and that at the same time people do not value water enough and are more likely to waste it.

In addition to the constraints imposed by the paucity of resources, other factors impaired the supply of water in the urban areas. Among these are: the lack of a proper urban development programme; inadequate water supply from some of the main tapping sources which serve the urban areas; and an estimated 40 percent leakage caused by an ancient and dilapidated infrastructure.

The government has prepared a draft sector policy for urban management, service delivery, and infrastructure investment, aimed at creating an effective institutional and financial framework for operating a sustainable service delivery system in urban centres. Municipalities have been given a greater voice in the management of urban water supply and sewerage through the opening in July 1994 of Special Funds, the appointment of Water Advisory Boards, and the creation of Urban Water and Sewerage Departments in three pilot towns.

As far as sanitation is concerned, the reality is that lack of financial resources has had a very negative impact on urban sanitation in Tanzania. For example, in 1985 and 1986 the city generated 1,200 tons of solid waste daily in Dar es Salaam city but had the capacity to collect only 10 percent of the garbage. In order to be able to remove all waste water, the city needed 150 emptiers during this period. However, until March 1988, the city had a total of only 23 cesspit emptiers. The continuation of a squeezed budget means that city and town councils are unable to maintain city cleanliness. As a result, uncollected garbage is widespread in urban areas, and overflowing pit latrines are the order of the day in squatter areas and/or settlements occupied by the poor. This kind of situation is making the urban environment an unhealthy place in which to live. The situation has worsened, as these are the same areas where informal economic activities have been concentrated in recent years. Finally, the situation has been aggravated by the deterioration in local administration and community based organization in the cities, especially Dar es Salaam.

Challenges

Most of the urban areas of Tanzania are experiencing a water crisis. This crisis is likely to intensify with the increase in urban population and an expansion of industrial manufacturing activities. In view of the decreasing ability of the government to finance public services after the economic reforms, the challenge to the urban water sector centres on designing a self-sustaining and efficient water supply system capable of supplying sufficient quantities of clean and reliable water to the households and enterprises in the urban areas. A further challenge is the articulation of appropriate water development programmes and pricing policies that emphasize economic rates (rather than flat rates) and user charges where it is very necessary to differentiate the market. It is also important to underscore that an efficient water supply system would require a properly trained and efficient management team, technical experts, etc. to market rather than "just sell or supply" water. Moreover, in view of the importance of water in human and non-human economic activity, a challenge that arises is to find the most appropriate and efficient ways to regulate and supervise the supply of water in the urban areas.

Policy options

The water sector policy of 1991 addressed sources, use of water in the urban areas, planning and quality of water supply, financing and maintenance of water operations, authorities responsible for water (such as NUWA and Regional Water Authorities), and enforcement and co-ordination policies of the water sector. The policy retained the long-term objective of making safe water available at a minimum cost, estimated at 20 to 30 litres per person per day, obtainable within 400m from a water kiosk which would serve about 200 to 250 people. According to this policy, water connection costs up to the plot boundary would be met by the water authority, and those within the plot boundary by the customer.

Short-term policy options

(a) There is a need to revamp the organizational structure of the water supply sector and improve the infrastructure in order to enhance efficiency and delivery of the service. This policy approach could be carried out along the lines of the Water and Sanitation Advisory Boards established for Tanga, Moshi, Arusha and Mwanza in 1995.

(b) Restructuring and capitalization of NUWA is necessary to improve its services.

(c) Consistent with the reforms adopted in other sectors of the economy, there appears to be a need to bestow the water-pricing task on NUWA and water authorities in the urban centres. In the same vein, it is important that the proportion of water revenues paid to the central government is reduced to aid the urban water departments to improve the quantity and quality of their services.

(d) Universal metering needs to be emphasized to ensure that the customer pays for the service supplied.

(e) It is necessary to put in place a regulatory and supervisory framework that would condition the adopted pricing policy on the customers' willingness to pay, "fair" return to the supplier, and environmental and government policies, etc.

(f) There is a need to establish performance indicators and, accordingly, reward the efficient water agencies.

(g)   There is a need to emphasize coordination amongst the different departments in the urban areas. This underscores the need for proper and well-coordinated urban plans as a prerequisite for an improvement in the supply of water.

Long-term policy options
(a) Private participation in the water sector should be encouraged.
(b) The recycling and development of own sources of water, such as tapping of rainwater, groundwater, etc., and water conservation should be encouraged in the urban areas.

Tourism

Current status

Tanzania is blessed with many attractions for tourism including wildlife, Mount Kilimanjaro, and beautiful beaches. There are many cultural and historical attractions as well, such as traditional *ngoma*s, and Zanzibar and other coastal towns whose sights show the interaction of East Africa with many ancient civilizations including the Romans, the Indians and the Middle East. People come from around the world to experience the uniqueness of Ngorongoro and the timelessness of Serengeti. Kilimanjaro Mountain and the opportunities of communicating with "the traditional gods" on Mawenzi Peak provide unparalleled mountain climbing opportunities. As of 1994, the National Park system had expanded to eleven, namely, Serengeti, Ruaha, Ngorongoro, Mikumi, Tarangire, Katavi, Kilimanjaro, Rubondo, Manyara, Arusha and Gombe Stream. Together with Ngorongoro Conservation Area, these parks cover an area of approximately 46,000 square kilometres and occupy about 5 percent of the total land area.

For nearly three decades after Tanzania's independence, tourism kept a very low profile. However, the National Tourism Policy, which was put in place in 1991, and the government policy of trade and economic liberalization have had a positive impact on the acceleration of tourism development. In 1994 about 262,000 tourists visited Tanzania.

Tanzania is among the ten most popular destinations for tourists in Africa. It also ranks among the countries with the highest receipt per tourist in Africa: US$733 per tourist. In 1993 it was ranked fourth in Africa. With an average length of stay in the country of seven days, it is highly ranked in sub-Saharan Africa but falls below Kenya, Seychelles and Ghana.

The liberalization of the economy and the creation of the IPC have had a positive impact on the growth of tourism in Tanzania. Private investors have moved in to provide capital for new hotels or to rehabilitate older hotels formerly owned and run by the state. In the coastal circuit the Sheraton Hotel is a new five-star hotel while a South African company has bought the New

Africa Hotel and is finalizing its rehabilitation and expansion. A good number of game lodges in the Northern Circuit have been acquired and are being rehabilitated by Sopa Limited and Serena Hotels.

Problems and challenges

Broadly speaking, the tourism product consists of two main components, namely, tourist attractions and human needs in respect of facilities and services. The latter refers to the basic infrastructure, which includes accommodation, roads, railways, telecommunications, good hospitals, transport, water supply, energy, and air transport. It is evident, therefore, that the country has exotic and unique attractions in abundance but not, strictly speaking, the product. Adequate infrastructure is crucial for the development of tourism. As in other export-oriented industries, Tanzania must try to establish a competitive edge in tourism in order to catch up with and move ahead of competitors. Rooms, meals, transport and other tourist services must be priced competitively.

Similarly, as in the other productive and commercial sectors where the government is increasingly disengaging from direct involvement and moving into coordination and regulation, lack of reliable data is a big hindrance towards accomplishing these new tasks. All kinds of hotels are being built, for example, but to date there are no grading systems and no guidelines for investors in tourist facilities.

Policy options

Policy formulation
Tourism policies in past years have not taken other related sectors into consideration. The lack of a multi-sectoral approach to tourism policies has negatively affected the established hotels in the Northern Circuit. Poor roads and telecommunications facilities have caused many disappointments to otherwise willing tourists.

Tourism mix
Traditionally, the development of tourism has been undertaken in isolation from the surroundings of the area. The culture of the communities, ecology, and environment should form a tourism mix. All policies should aim at facilitating the development of the tourism mix elements. Tourism must be culturally responsible, ecologically friendly and environmentally sustainable. The development of one element to the detriment of the other elements in the tourism mix has far reaching repercussions in the industry.

Classification of hotels

In both the short and long-term, it should be the rule rather than the exception to classify hotels so that any prospective hotel owner knows what contribution is expected of him or her. The way hotels are mushrooming in various towns will only contribute to the creation of substandard quality tourism. For instance, Kariakoo is notorious for cheap hotels and guesthouses. Without classification and standardization of services, promotion becomes a haphazard business. The current laissez-faire attitude of hotel establishments hurts tourist business.

Human Resource Development

Tanzania seems to take its wildlife attractions and hotel industry for granted without applying a critical eye to the skills of the personnel required to run them. Mweka Wildlife College has catered for conservation efforts, but nothing of the same level is in place anywhere in Tanzania for hotel management, except for the modest attempts by private initiative, such as the Bismark Hotel Training School. The 500,000 tourists hoped for per year thus currently pass through the hands of semi-skilled hotel personnel.

Tourism development creates jobs at various levels, hence the need to have a proper training school similar to Kenya's Utalii College. Upgrading Forodhani Hotel and Tourism Training Institute or simply establishing a higher level college with a comprehensive tourism syllabus would augur well for the sustainable tourism development that has been given lip service for so long.

This chapter examines the status of the social sectors and their challenges and policy options in general. In particular, it addresses major problems and policy issues in health, in education and in the social aspects of water and sanitation.

General issues

Current status

For its level of development Tanzania has made considerable progress in improving its people's access to basic social services. The thrust has been on the development of education, health, nutrition and water and sanitation services.

Progress in the delivery of social services was rapid in the 1960s and 1970s but encountered setbacks in the 1980s. The delivery of social services could not be sustained because the productive base was weakening in the late 1970s and 1980s and mechanisms for sharing the responsibilities of investments and operations in the social sectors had not been put in place. The government carried this responsibility largely on its own. The collapse of self-help schemes and the dismantling or erosion of local government and community level institutions, coupled with restrictions on private sector participation and the promises that the villagization programme would be accompanied by free access to social services, meant that the responsibility for meeting investment and recurrent costs in the social sector was largely left to the government. The government could not sustain the levels of success that had been reached by the end of the 1970s.

Persistent budgetary constraints have led to major policy and strategic changes, the objective being to revitalize and accelerate development in the social sector. In all sectors (education, health and water and sanitation) restriction on private sector participation has been removed, greater beneficiary involvement in planning and managing of facilities is being promoted and cost-sharing has been introduced. Along with mechanisms for ensuring accessibility of the poor to basic services there is also greater emphasis on cost effectiveness in the provision of care. Recently, a social sector strategy that, among other things, emphasizes decentralization of decision-making powers to local authorities and coordination across sectors has been prepared and is being tested. This is intended to provide a framework for coordinated action in the social sectors.

Special attention is still required to encourage greater participation of local level institutions and to set up appropriate mechanisms for ensuring accessibility by the poor to basic social services.

Outstanding challenges and problems

The social sector is facing challenges related to underfunding, inadequate coordination (e.g., education with health and sanitation, or housing with sanitation), an over-centralized management system, skewed allocation of resources (especially in favour of urban areas), and unclear prioritization (e.g., allocation of resources to new projects or on-going projects). The government has prepared a new Education and Training Policy (approved by Cabinet) and a proposal for Health Sector Reform. The basic problems addressed by these policies have been summarized by the government's Social Sector Strategy. Pilot projects have been developed to test new approaches to financing basic health, education and water services. These projects depend heavily on increasing accountability of those services to their clients by putting control over public subsidies closer to households. Districts, rather than the central government, now set the minimum primary school fees and proceeds stay with the school.

Policy options

The institutional capacity for planning and management of the social sectors needs to be strengthened and the respective roles and responsibilities of different levels need to be clarified. Coordination in planning and management is necessary between the centre, line ministries, and local government. Because of lack of adequate coordination and communication these do tend to look at issues differently. Specifically, their roles and responsibilities, especially between the Prime Minister's Office (PMO) (local government) and the line Ministries are either confusing or are being ignored by PMO. The line Ministries are the "professional" Ministries, while the Prime Minister's Office is the "operator" of basic services.

On the grounds of social equity and social returns, government funding should be more devoted to primary and secondary education and primary health care. Private resources should be mobilized to support tertiary and specialized services. The bottom-up budgetary process must end up at district level.

Constraints to private sector participation in provision of social services must be eliminated. Those who want to invest in the rural areas must be encouraged to do so through special incentives. Detailed regulations on this must continue to be worked out, especially at local levels.

The quality of education and health in the country is on the decline. Essential inputs are lacking and delivery is inefficient. In addition, perception of poor quality has apparently affected demand as enrolment ratios, in education for example, have declined. In the short to medium-term there is urgent need to improve the inputs and the process of social services delivery. Personnel must be supported by adequate resources. Many more materials (drugs, supplies, textbooks, teaching aids, etc.) are needed, and effective systems for their procurement and distribution should be put in place. Equally important is the ongoing maintenance and rehabilitation of the existing physical facilities. Expansion plans for the provision of social services must be based on realistic assumptions on resource mobilization and social demand. Reforms in the social sectors must be normal and constant practice.

Education

Current status

In education, the quantity and quality of education services offered have declined. In recent years the literacy rates have decreased, the primary enrolment rate has fallen, and performance in examinations deteriorated until 1994, with only a small improvement in 1995.

The literacy rate has decreased from 90 percent in 1986 to 84 percent in 1992. Data from the 1993/94 Human Resource and Development Survey (HRDS) indicate that the self-reported illiteracy rate is twice as high as the official rate. If this estimate is correct the literacy level is only 68 percent.

The primary school gross enrolment rate has stagnated at around 74 percent and the net enrolment rate at 53 percent. At secondary education level, only five percent of eligible children are enrolled. This is the lowest rate in the world. The drop out rate is high, especially among female students. The high rate of drop out is due to a range of reasons, including poor quality of education, inability by some parents to provide uniforms, fees and other contributions, teenage pregnancy and early marriage for girls. Some parents simply do not appreciate education.

The declining trend in examination performance at form four and six levels indicates that the quality of education at both primary and secondary level has deteriorated in recent years. At form four level the proportion of students passing at division I fell from 7.7 percent in 1990 to a mere 2.9 percent in 1994, and rose by just 0.6 percent to 3.5 percent in 1995. Meanwhile, the proportion of students passing at division IV level increased between 1990 and 1994, rising from 42 percent to 57.2 percent, before dropping slightly to 55.3 percent in 1995. The trend is similar at form six level, where division I pass rates fell from 16 percent in 1990 to 4.7 percent in 1994 before rising to 5.2 percent in 1995. Division IV passes increased from 11.1 in 1990 to 23.3 in 1994, before dropping to 20.7 in 1995.[7] This improvement in examination results is slight, and the extent to which pass rates had dropped by 1994 has very serious implications for the quality of education in Tanzania.

Although the national teacher/pupil ratio at primary school level is one teacher to 40 pupils, about 63 percent of primary school teachers are not adequately qualified (their qualifications lie below grade A). Also, the distribution of teachers at primary and secondary school levels is very uneven, with some areas having more teachers than required and others experiencing severe shortages.

Outstanding challenges and problems

(a) In education, declining primary school enrolment rates and high drop out rates at all levels of the education system pose a special challenge to the government.
(b) Limited capacity at secondary level is a major problem (and challenge) especially in a situation of limited resources and increasing demand.
(c) High drop out rates and limited accessibility among girls and children from poor households is another issue which needs close government attention, especially when cost-sharing is being emphasized as a means of increasing resources to education.

Policy options

The government should immediately organize itself to implement the education and training policy that has been prepared by the Ministry of Education and Culture. The Ministry of Science and Technology and Higher Education is in the process of preparing its policy. Coordination between the two ministries on this matter is practically non-existent.

The most sensitive area in education is textbooks on which, along with teachers' abilities, the quality of education hangs. Whoever controls this area is in command of the education sector and for several years now it has been dominated by the Swedish International Development Agency (SIDA). They control almost everything, including the process of liberalizing this sub-sector. The government should take measures to phase out dependence on donor resources and power in this area.

Some of the problems facing basic education have their causes and roots in the ministry itself. The government should take immediate stock of the people managing the Ministry of Education and Culture. Dynamism and innovation are not common there. Without a good foundation of manpower and without vision at the ministry level, the education sector will continue to suffer.

Health

Current status

In the health sector, each upper level of the health care system is supposed to deal with referral cases from the level immediately below it. If the referral system functions as required, with a network of 183 hospitals, 291 health centres and 3,286 dispensaries, it is estimated that about 93 percent of the people live within 10 km of a health facility, while 72 percent are within five km of a health facility. But given the shortage of drugs and other essential supplies in public facilities, it appear that many people still travel long distances in search of better services. Resource allocation in health is skewed in favour of tertiary hospital services, urban areas and salaries. The current observed shortages of drugs and essential medical supplies is partly a result of this imbalance. With respect to personnel, allocation is biased in favour of urban areas. On the preventive-curative services balance, in spite of government emphasis on preventive care, a recent analysis of government expenditure indicates that 77.9 percent of government resources are spent on curative care.[8] Preventive care takes only 15.4 percent, mostly from donors, and community health takes about 6.6 percent. In spite of the fact that some preventive activities take place in other sectors, this is an indication that the emphasis on preventive care has not been adequately translated into action.

There appears to be over dependence on donor support for the supply of drugs and other essential medical supplies. For example, nearly all drugs used in public facilities are imported by donors, notably the Danish International Development Agency (DANIDA). This may imply that the supply of drugs and other essential inputs can be sustained only as long as donors are willing to support the health care system.

Private medical practice is even more skewed in favour of urban areas and the expansion of its activities has not been accompanied by appropriate regulatory mechanisms to ensure adherence to medical ethics. This is one aspect that deserves greater attention.

Outstanding challenges and problems

(a)   The emergence and rapid spread of AIDS poses a special health problem. Even the modest gains made over the past three decades are likely to be reversed in the next few years if the epidemic continues to spread at current rates.

(b)   The recent introduction of cost-sharing has created accessibility problems for some sections of the population, especially the poor who are estimated to make up about 50 percent of the population.

(c)   Lack of awareness of the causes of some health problems is a major challenge. Most problems could be eliminated if the people were adequately informed about their causes.

Policy options

The quality and availability of health services in the country are severely constrained by shortages of medical supplies and equipment. This is another sensitive area. Whoever dominates this sub-sector dominates the entire sector. For many years, this has been the domain of DANIDA. In this area, the government should take measures to phase out dependence and regain control. The government should allocate enough funds for drugs but it should also encourage private importation for private buying. In addition, the government should regulate health care so that the public can be assured that private providers will provide high quality, affordable and accessible health care.

Health facilities are in poor physical condition. Buildings are decaying, water and electrical supplies are out of order, and sanitation measures are often non-functional. This makes for unpleasant and unhealthy working conditions for staff and adversely affects the quality of services received by patients. Besides the government, local participation is very important to rectify the situation. Priority should be given to Primary Health Care facilities that provide greater access to the population. The fact that Primary Health Care will continue to be the main strategy means that the major source of financing will be the public sector.

As a short and long-term measure, the health sector should have people at district and regional levels who appreciate data collection, and are able to analyze it and to make it usable at these levels. General health education, which is currently underplayed, must be effectively promoted.

Community participation is very important. Households and communities determine health behaviours and make key decisions about the use of health services. Any sustainable initiative in health services must therefore respond to their needs. This includes setting priorities, planning and managing health services.

An important component of any strategy to improve the quality and impact of health care must reach beyond the health authorities: a multi-sectoral approach is needed. It is therefore important for the health sector to augment communications with those in other sectors, taking advantage of the commonality of their goals by sharing ideas and possibly resources. This is particularly important during the planning, monitoring and evaluation stages.

Nutrition

Current status

In Tanzania, the major nutritional problems are Protein Energy Malnutrition, Nutritional Anaemia, Iodine Deficiency Disorders and Vitamin A Deficiency. These mostly affect children under 5 years and pregnant and lactating mothers.

Nutritional problems are mainly due to the following two important causes:

(a) inadequate food intake resulting from low feeding frequency with insufficient energy and other important nutrients, a problem that usually affects children, and
(b) the frequent incidence of diseases such as malaria, worms, bilharzia, diarrhoea, etc.

Outstanding challenges

As with health problems, lack of awareness among the people about the causes of some nutritional problems is a major challenge to nutrition managers.

Policy options

Management of malnutrition should be decentralized to focus on the district. Each district should collect information on nutrition/ malnutrition and develop strategies to improve the situation. Vertical programmes must be minimized.

Water and sanitation (as a social factor)

Current status

The Tanzania Water Supply System is structured on a rural-urban basis. No fee is charged on rural water supply services apart from a small contribution by beneficiaries in some places for minor repairs and maintenance requirement. The 1991 water policy emphasizes more beneficiary responsibility in running rural water schemes. Urban water supply is provided on a user fee basis. However, due to ineffective fee collection and low tariffs, revenue is lower than operating costs.

Official estimates indicate a rural and urban coverage of 46 and 67 percent respectively in 1993. These statistics further indicate variation in coverage rates between regions. An unspecified number of schemes were operating below capacity due to a range of reasons including inadequate supply of recurrent inputs. While effective coverage appears to be much lower than officially estimated, available data further indicates that supply is far below demand.

The problems of waste water and sewage have already been mentioned in Chapter Three. Only eight towns in mainland Tanzania have limited sewerage systems. In these towns, some of the few households with flush toilets are connected to the sewer system; others empty into septic tanks and soakways. As a result, most pit latrines are not regularly emptied. Even where emptier trucks are available, they often deposit refuse and garbage without treatment to specified points. Estimates further indicate that only 20 percent of garbage is collected in urban areas. Storm water drainage is also very poor, leading to regular flooding in most urban areas during the rainy seasons. The poor condition of sanitation could be a main cause of diseases such as diarrhoea. This is one area where primary health care could make a difference.

Outstanding challenges and problems

(a) Destruction of water sources is a major cause of the failure of many water schemes. In spite of frequently expressed concern by the Ministry of Water, Energy and Minerals, the problems appear to be escalating. Without gaining control of this problem, the goal of water for all by the year 2010 may not be attained.

(b) The range of technologies used in the provision of water makes cost containment difficult as operating and maintenance costs vary from one technology to another. The challenge here is to determine and institutionalize the type of technology that is most cost effective.

Policy options

Rural water supplies must continue to be given high priority. Safe water is very important for the achievement of social welfare. Villagers must continue to be given training for maintenance of water schemes. Appropriate, simple and affordable technology must be used and water funds must continue to be encouraged. The private sector should be allowed and encouraged to operate emptier trucks in order to alleviate the current shortage.

This chapter addresses those issues which cut across several sectors of the economy. The issues examined here include the export sector, science and technology, the evironment, human resource development and employment, women in development, child survival, protection and development, civil service reform, parastatal sector reform, the role of the state, external resource inflow and regional and international cooperation.

Export sector

Current status

Despite ten years of economic policy reform efforts, including the implementation of Structural Adjustment Programmes (SAPs), Tanzania still faces balance of payments problems. Credit items in Tanzania's current account, such as exports, do not provide enough foreign exchange to generate the revenues necessary to augment domestic revenue sources, to expand domestic savings, to finance imports and to service external debt, including the payment of interest and principal. Dependence on foreign aid as a source of foreign savings without a massive increase in export receipts cannot put a low-income country like Tanzania on a new growth path. Given Tanzania's continued dependence on imports for investment and current production, an export push is essential in order to finance the required imports and to augment the country's resources. In particular emphasis should be given to non-traditional exports, including services. One of the promising services is tourism, as described in Chapter 4. Yet tourism contributes only 1.4 percent to the GDP and brings in about 10 percent of our foreign exchange earnings. These figures show that the potential for tourism has not been exploited to the fullest.

Tanzania also has an opportunity to increase exports of many other products apart from traditional exports, minerals, and tourism. Among these products are canned fruits and vegetables of various types. The statistical estimates show that Tanzania produces over 3000 metric tonnes of fruits and vegetables each year, much of which remains unharvested or ends up being thrown away because of lack of a market. Other potential exports could consist of livestock products, as Tanzania ranks third in Africa in terms of the size of livestock resources. In 1991, for example, the country was estimated to have 14 million head of cattle, and 12 million sheep and goats.

About 50 percent of Tanzania's land is covered by forest, mainly savanna and intermediate woodlands suitable for production of high quality forestry products. Within the forests, populations of wild honeybees are found, which could enable the development of bee keeping activities and hence production of honey, beeswax, and other products that have a large export market.

Tanzania is also endowed with substantial resources for the development of a fishing industry. Blessed with some of the largest freshwater lakes in the world (Lakes Victoria, Nyasa, and Tanganyika), as well as a long coastline on the Indian Ocean, and a good number of rivers of different sizes, the country has considerable potential for developing a modern fishing and fish canning industry for domestic and export markets.

The facts and figures below sum up Tanzania's foreign trade status as of 1995.

(a)   World trade has doubled since 1980, while Tanzanian trade has remained relatively stagnant.

(b)   Tanzania's exports were valued at US$440 million in 1993 (US$553.7 million in 1981 while the country's imports in the same year were valued at US$1.5 billion.

(c)   Total exports (formal and informal) may be as much as three times the official figure of approximately US$500 million, and total imports may approach US$3 billion. Currently, virtually all Tanzanian gold and approximately 90 percent of its gemstones are exported via non-formal channels. The annual value of these informal exports is estimated at US$115 million for gold and about US$70 million for gemstones.

(d)   Tanzania's current account balance deficit, before official transfers, was US$948 million in 1993.

(e)   Tanzania is the most indebted nation in Eastern Africa. Export earnings can cover only 6.3 percent of this debt. Total debt service alone accounted for 27 percent of export earnings in 1993.

Coffee exports in 1994 declined in volume to 37,000 tonnes, the lowest level since 1973. Coffee export value, however, increased to US$115.4 million, the highest value since 1986, when it was US$184 million. Coffee prices in 1994 almost doubled compared to 1993. Tanzania coffee yields have been declining since 1987: 4.4 tonnes per hectare (tph) were harvested in 1993 compared to 5.2 tph in 1987, while tea yields are at the same level as in 1986 (11.1 tph).

Cotton yields have recently improved (5.5 tph) but are still below the 1989 peak of 5.9 tph. Cotton exports in 1994 amounted to 60,000 tonnes, a decline from the 72,800 tonnes exported in 1992, which was the peak export year for cotton in the last twenty years. Cotton export value in 1994 amounted to US$105.1 million, the highest ever in the two decades, due to a remarkable increase in cotton prices, which offset the decline in production.

Raw cashew nut exports boomed in 1994 to 65,000 tonnes from 32,200 tonnes in 1993, with revenues increasing from US$23.3 million to US$51.2 million.

Tanzania's non-traditional exports have, in 1994, been slightly lower than in 1993 (US$182.5 million and US$183.7 million respectively). Export of minerals has decreased by half from US$ 69 million in 1993 to US$30 million in 1994, largely due to increased smuggling, particularly of gold and gemstones.

Exports of manufactured goods increased to US$77 million in 1994 from US$52 million in 1993 but are still far from the twenty-year peak of US$105 million in 1989. The industrial sector is affected by low capacity utilization partly caused by problems of obsolete technology, declining markets in the face of competition with imported products, and financial constraints. In addition, disruptions in the supply of core infrastructure, particularly electricity, have resulted in further production losses.

Challenges

To improve resource availability and the country's creditworthiness and to augment savings, etc., the expansion of exports is crucial. However, as is well known, production and trade of primary commodities have not grown as fast as world income because of low-income elasticity of demand for most primary commodities. Reasons behind the declining demand for primary commodities include a decline in raw material use, technological change, changes in taste, blending with synthetics, and competition from synthetic substitutes. But demand has in some cases grown rapidly for some primary commodities such as fresh fruit, vegetable oils, shrimp and fish. Given this scenario, it is important for countries such as Tanzania to diversify their exports and to begin tapping immediately this export potential for non-traditional export commodities.

The lesson for Tanzania is to quickly diversify into non-traditional exports where a minimum of prior investment is needed in order to start producing. There is no possibility of failure from such a move of export diversification once quality standards are adhered to. There are countries with large primary commodity sectors that diversified and managed to achieve impressive growth rates including Chile, Malaysia and Thailand to mention just a few.

Other benefits of export promotion are that:

(a) it raises investment efficiency, resulting in the improved allocation of resources

(b) it provides strong incentives to producers to be efficient in the use of factors of production, to keep production costs low, to innovate, to improve and maintain high quality standards, and to sustain high rates of investment, as a result of international competitive pressure

(c)   it shifts the distribution of income in favour of the factors of production employed in the export sector

(d)   it enables a labour-abundant economy such as Tanzania to concentrate growth in employment-intensive activities (coffee, cotton, cashew, tea, fruit, flower and vegetable production and harvesting/picking, small scale mineral extraction, fishing, etc.), which can lead to the raising of real wages and improvement in income distribution as happened in Malaysia and Mauritius among a number of other countries

(e)   it leads to rapid growth of the GDP, and

(f)   it helps to reduce indebtedness, thus improving a country's creditworthiness.

It is important to note that even in a case where the "adding-up problem" is applicable (i.e., there is little scope for increased gains from a massive export drive for primary commodities), a country can still improve her gains from exports via improving efficiency in production, processing and marketing. Indeed, in the case of Tanzania a lot more could be gained by simply improving efficiency in production, processing and marketing of current potential and actual output levels for coffee, cotton, cashews and tea.

There is also a need to strengthen certain policy measures as well as institutional arrangements, in order to both implement a major export-drive initiative and gain from export growth. Taking a cue from the experience of East Asia, Tanzania must promote export growth via export incentives, via putting in place the requisite export infrastructure, via upgrading market/exporting capabilities, via the provisioning of export credits and technical assistance directed towards exporters, via ensuring that the exchange rate is not over-valued, etc.

Commodity prices are not expected to improve in the foreseeable future and there are no immediate gains to be had from engaging in complaining or blaming the unfavourable terms of trade and international trading arrangements. We need to shift gear by coming up with innovative ideas on how to diversify and break out of the "traditional commodity syndrome" or overdependence on a few traditional commodities or even lamenting Tanzania's "lost glories" in the sisal crop. Tanzania is endowed with ample arable land (of which less than 25 percent is used productively); a high mineral resource potential (diamonds, gold, nickel, cobalt, gemstones, natural gas, etc.); marine resources (shrimp, prawns, fish, etc.); and a number of non-traditional export commodities like flowers, fruits, and oilseeds. Why shouldn't Tanzania make it? What does it take to make a breakthrough in export growth?

Compared to many African countries, Tanzania has a diversified export structure. Yet her export performance is not satisfactory and could easily be doubled with minimal prior investment requirement. Indeed, considering Tanzania's population size, availability of natural resources, size of arable land that could support a flourishing agriculture-based export growth, marine resources (rivers, lakes and the Indian Ocean) and mineral resources potential, it is quite obvious that Tanzania is producing well below her potential output levels. Tanzania's total export earnings are about one third of those of neighbouring Kenya. And, whereas in 1980 Tanzania's total exports were slightly larger than those of Mauritius, by 1992 Mauritius' exports were 3.3 times those of Tanzania. Tanzania is fortunate to have a diversified export structure that can foster significant leaps in export performance. The problem is really not the lack of exportable produce but rather the problem of poor export promotion and inadequate facilitation of the efficient production of traditional export commodities, and non-traditional export commodities and minerals.

The challenges in developing the tourist industry are great if the country's potential is to be exploited. A major challenge is the investment in the supportive infrastructure (roads, tours, communications, hotels). In order to substantially increase forex earnings from tourism, the country has to facilitate the development of tourist attractions and to target key markets for construction of infrastructure such as access roads, water supply, electricity, airstrips and telecommunications. This requires putting in place a tourism development policy that will encourage investment in the necessary supportive infrastructure.

Policy options

A lot needs to be done for Tanzania to make the most of her export potential. On the institutional arrangement level, fundamental changes are urgently needed in the structure and functioning of those government departments (such as the directorate of external trade in the Ministry of Industries and Trade) and other public institutions charged with the responsibility of export promotion (such as the Board of External Trade, and the Tanzania Tourist Board). Various institutions related to export promotion need personnel who can perform and produce results. They also need strengthening in terms of how they operate (i.e., removal of unnecessary red tape from umbrella or parent institutions and promotion of autonomy where necessary).

To develop a successful export programme, free and accessible trade-related information, including information on the requisite quality standards, should be provided to the various key players and interested parties. Such information should not only be available in the capital city but also in the various regional and district centres that have export potential. Needless to say, such information needs to be found under one roof. Currently such information is not readily available and, when accessible, is costly in terms of effort, time, and even money (travel expenses, telephone inquiries, etc.).

Emphasis must be shifted from economy wide price policies to the missing non-price links. On the supply side of exports, special attention should be given to adequate provision of appropriate institutions, infrastructure, inputs, information and innovations. On the demand side of exports, various aspects of non-price competition will deserve greater attention, for example, the marketing and excellence of the products.

Apart from enhancing potential to produce, issues of quality, reliability, dependability and a competitive supply price need to be observed. Not only should the export commodities meet stringent quality control standards but they should also have predictable delivery arrangements so that the trading houses in the importing countries can conduct a predictable business. A trading environment characterized by intermittent deliveries and inconsistent quality standards does not help, and in fact hurts, a country's chances of getting the most out of exports.

As explained above, to carry out a successful export-drive initiative, certain export supporting infrastructure systems must be in place, including telecommunications, roads, railways, airports, ports, etc. Since most of these infrastructures have been run-down since the late 1970s a major rehabilitation drive should be initiated and in some cases completely new systems should be constructed. The state should play a role in stimulating investments in this construction. In particular, it should put in place a policy framework that is conducive to attracting such investments. Other necessary infrastructure and services include warehouses and export finance/credit schemes. Over and above having functioning and efficient infrastructure support systems, it is important to have a stable and predictable policy on exports.

Besides creating the requisite institutions to facilitate export growth, it is important to ensure that these institutions function properly and serve to promote export growth. In this regard, Tanzania must have a system of intervention and close supervision in order to promote its exports effectively.

A comprehensive market strategy will need to be put in place through participation in exhibitions, and through embassies and agent representation. In this regard, Tanzania's embassies have a greater role to play in promoting the country's export products and tourist attractions. To ensure this, each Tanzanian embassy should have a trade attaché who is well-versed in commercial or trade matters, whose role is to "sell" the country and explore market potentials for the country's products. Within the country, the numbers of locally trained personnel for the tourist industry should be increased, as discussed in Chapter 4.

Science and technology (S&T)

Current status

The weakness of technological management capacities in the less advanced developing countries deprives them of the new opportunities for development progress. In a world where the pace of technological change and its impact on world supply and demand patterns are intensifying, they face grave risks of falling further behind the rest of the world in their income-generating and problem-solving potential, while at the same time they have to contend with intensified demographic, economic and environmental change. Against this background, strengthening the national capacity of these countries to manage technological change should be regarded as a central and urgent development issue.

The basic issues are now much more clearly defined as broad development management issues requiring a close partnership between the S&T community, the economic and social policy makers, and the general public in order to define orientations and processes that will direct S&T resources to advancing broad-based economic development. This will involve the promotion of a national dialogue engaging all relevant stakeholders in the development process (including politicians, business people in all sectors, professional groups, voluntary organizations, public administrators, etc.) in the process of managing technological change. They must also take account of physical, social and political factors that require particular attention, such as the environment, the role of women, and the needs of specially disadvantaged groups.

Challenges

The world is in a process of rapid transition in which political alignments, economic systems and social values are being transformed. It is increasingly being recognized that at the base of these changes is the acceleration of scientific and technological advances, which has had a strong influence on the manner of building up desirable human resources. The challenge facing Tanzania, in this context, is to enlarge the capacity of its people so that they can benefit from the advances of science and technology in securing a better life. The educational system should be able to instill a technology culture from its earliest levels. The establishment of a strong industrial base will certainly require specialized and diversified training at the tertiary level together with an educational system that stresses the pursuit of vocational and technical studies. This, in turn, will require a strong foundation in the science bias at primary and secondary levels.

The promotion of entrepreneurship requires that educational and other government policies encourage managerial and business skills. Technological input as well as technical knowledge should reinforce these. The educational system must therefore be orientated towards the production of graduates who are employment creators rather than employment seekers. The need for training and re-training of human capital is a prerequisite in order to improve productivity and to march in step with the rapid changes in science and technology.

Policy options

The links between academia, R&D institutions and industry need to be revisited with a view to reducing the gaps and strengthening collaboration between and among them. R&D institutions should be restructured to reflect the needs of users more effectively, and users should be better informed about the activities and capabilities of R&D institutions. In this connection it will be important to set up an incentive structure that will encourage enterprises to continue searching for technological improvements based on their own efforts, and those of the local R&D institutions and technology sources in other countries.

In order to meet the basic needs of the people, Tanzania must harness science and technology and develop its international competitiveness in the selected export activities. The balance between these two objectives has to be addressed, especially in the context of global economic liberalization and rapid technological advancement. Nevertheless, in some developing countries little or no attention has been paid to redressing this imbalance in the S&T policies. Comprehensive S&T policy reviews would help not only to set such policy in the context of broader development and economic policies, but hopefully also to enable a balance to be achieved. The implementation strategy of the S&T policy should be integrated into overall national socio-economic planning. All stakeholders in the development process should be involved in the preparation of the strategy.

In order to accord science and technology its central role in national development, it is important to ensure that effective institutional frameworks and linkages are established at various levels. It is recommended that a high-powered independent national S&T advisory committee be established to keep the President of Tanzania abreast of science and technology issues. The President should also have a science and technology advisor. Various committees on science and technology should be established at different levels, namely: cabinet, inter-ministerial (technical), parliamentary (already formed), ministerial, regional, district and the village. The committees will be responsible for the analysis of the science and technology needs, pinpointing where emphasis should be placed, which resources are required, etc. Institutions charged with the development, promotion, monitoring and coordination of science and technology have to work functionally and structurally as a system geared towards the optimal use of resources to achieve the objectives. The ministry responsible for science and technology should be a central one with the overall mandate of overseeing S&T and R&D institutions in the country.

Creation of institutional mechanisms for the development of networking/ partnership at all levels (national, regional and international) supported by the private and public sectors should be accorded high priority. Substantial evidence indicates that the efforts of small and medium scale enterprises (SMEs) to pool their resources, information, technologies and skills have often had a positive impact on their competitiveness and industrial efficiency. Firms will need to analyze (or be provided with support services to analyze) their domestic environment and to assess potential partnerships with a view to capitalizing on complementarity in the partnerships they establish with other (local and foreign) firms. [9]

Much of the current thinking on environmental protection focuses on what to do with wastes and emissions after they have been created—the traditional end-of-pipe approach. The goal of cleaner production is to avoid generating waste in the first place, and to minimize the use of raw materials and energy. In the long run, cleaner production is the most cost-effective way to operate processes and to develop and produce products. The costs of wastes and emissions, in addition to the negative environmental and health impacts, can be avoided by applying the cleaner production concept. Cleaner production, which was strongly endorsed in Agenda 21, helps industry and governments develop their competitive edge. The government should support the newly established Cleaner Production Centre of Tanzania (CPCT) in coordinating, facilitating and monitoring activities related to cleaner production and environmentally sound technology throughout the country.

The government should expedite the process of putting into operation the Patent Act No. 1 of 1987. This act makes better provisions for the promotion of inventiveness and innovation for facilitation of the acquisition of science and technology on fair terms and conditions through the grant and regulation of patents, utility and innovation certificates. Close follow-up should be made on the developments of Trade Related Intellectual Property (TRIP) and stakeholders kept informed. The patent registration office should be strengthened and encouraged to create awareness on the patent law within the society.

Environment

Current status

While deliberating on poverty assessment in Tanzania, it is necessary once again to reiterate the fact that sustainable economic development cannot be achieved without paying adequate attention to the quality of the environment. It is from environmental resources, such as forests, plains, mountains, wetlands and marine habitats, that the majority of low income rural and indeed even urban Tanzanians depend for food, fodder, firewood, game meat, building poles, timber, fish, medicinal plants and a wide variety of other products to sustain their lives. There is an important economic and social dimension to this that must be recognized.

In addition to direct values, the various ecosystems found in the country provide critical functions such as watershed protection, photosynthesis, regulation of climate and the production of soil. But these values are not yet captured in our systems of national accounts as benefits, nor do we consider them as costs when the environment is so degraded as to deny them to us.

The livelihood patterns of the growing number of households both in rural and urban areas provide us with indisputable evidence of the growing extent to which people depend on the natural environment for meeting their basic needs. Thus, if the quality of the environment suffers, this places those people in jeopardy and widespread poverty is likely to be exacerbated. This implies that the prospects for sound and sustainable economic growth and development will be limited and frustrated. The converse is also true, as access to adequate land, fertile soils, fodder, adequate and clean water, fuel wood, etc., form the essential building blocks for a better quality of life for the majority of Tanzanians.

Outstanding problems and issues

Tanzania is confronting a whole series of environmental problems that have rendered its socio-economic development unsustainable, to say the least. Proclaiming any economic success that does not take into account the persistent deterioration of the environmental quality in the country is unrealistic. Many of the environmental problems in Tanzania have economic and demographic manifestations thus these two parameters have to be brought into line with an urgent and practical environmental policy. There are six main areas of concern which need to be addressed immediately.

(a)   Land degradation is reducing the productivity of soils in many parts of Tanzania.

(b) Despite considerable national effort, over half the people in towns and the countryside do not have access to good quality water for washing, cooking, drinking and bathing.

(c) Pollution in towns and the countryside is affecting the health of many people and lowering the productivity of the environment.

(d) The loss of habitats for wildlife is threatening the national heritage and creating an uncertain future for the tourist industry.

(e) The productivity of lake, coastal and river waters is threatened by pollution and poor management.

(f) Tanzania's forest and woodland heritage is being reduced year by year through clearance for agriculture, for wood fuel and for other demands.

Policy options

The National Environmental Action Plan (NEAP) of July 1994 is a first step towards formulating a comprehensive environment policy. The government has finalized and endorsed the National Environmental Action Plan: A First Step, which was the result of broad-based participation involving government agencies, the private sector, NGOs, local communities and academia. A framework environmental law is in preparation.

The aim of the NEAP is to "achieve sustainable development that maximizes the long-term welfare of both present and future generations of Tanzanian people". A series of broad objectives follows this goal and they include:

(a) ensuring sustainable and equitable use of resources for meeting the basic needs of the present and future generations without degrading the environment or risking health and safety

(b) preventing and controlling degradation of land, water, vegetation and air which constitute our life support systems

(c) conserving and enhancing natural and man-made heritage, including the biological diversity of the unique ecosystems of Tanzania

(d) improving the condition and productivity of degraded areas including rural and urban settlements so that all Tanzanians may live in safe, healthful productivity and aesthetically pleasing surroundings

(e) raising public awareness and understanding of the essential linkages between environment and development and promoting individual and community participation in environmental action, and

(f) promoting international cooperation on the environmental agenda, and expanding our participation and contribution to relevant bilateral, subregional, regional and global organizations and programmes, including implementation of conventions.

Recognizing the need for direct action to help conserve Tanzania's natural resources and environment for sustainable growth, the government intended to implement an action plan based on the recently adopted NEAP. The government was determined to finalize and adopt the draft National Environment Policy by March 1996 and to define the government agency responsible for its implementation. In addition, by December 1996 the government wanted to establish a legislative framework articulated in the NEAP, prepare a priority long-term investment programme, and change policies to ensure that the prices of non-renewable resources reflect their true cost. Moreover, during this period, the government intended to strengthen institutional capacity to implement environmental programmes, improve the royalty collection system, produce a national land use and natural resource map, and develop a natural resource information centre.

To realize sustainable economic and social development while ameliorating the environmental damage that has already occurred and keeping at bay the whole range of existing environmental degradation, the government must legislate a transitional environmental policy and economic development programmes that take into account, inter alia, the following issues.

(a)   The projected environmental scenarios are often not as simple and straightforward as they may seem. The issues and causal factors are intrinsically complex. Therefore there is need to examine the physical, social, demographic, economic and political aspects of environmental issues in depth in order to understand what must be done to realize sustainable economic development.

(b)   An appropriate population policy that takes into account the positive and negative implications of population and its interaction with the environment needs to be formulated. As noted earlier, population alone is not the major problem. A poor population deprived of capital, education and technology within a constraining economic environment tends to have a significant impact on the environment, as people compete for limited resources. Poverty forces people to focus on short-term needs at the expense of long-term issues such as sustainable development and conservation of life support systems.

(c)   Regarding the environmental impact of agricultural growth, particularly the movement of the population from high to low yield areas, the government must influence this movement to where agriculture can be less damaging and more sustainable and productive. This implies the development of settlements in areas that are environmentally favourable and stable, which can be implemented through the provision of appropriate physical and social infrastructure in designated priority areas. In arid and semi-arid areas, where agro-pastoralism activities are on the increase, some limitations should be placed on these activities. In addition, appropriate areas with better potential and where a rotational system can be sustained should be identified and designated.

(d) Deforestation, caused by the harvesting of natural woodlands and by the invasion of watershed areas, results in topsoil loss and leads to erosion. Such practices threaten biodiversity and increase the threat of desertification. To remedy such negative trends natural resource management programmes and environmental action plans are needed such as those being practised under SECAP in the Usambaras. Exploitation limits should be on the basis of agro-ecological zones. Reserves need to be established in areas where deforestation is affecting watershed areas, accelerating soil erosion and contributing to a considerable loss of biodiversity husbandry methods for farmers.

(e) The pursuit of development will always have an impact on land and vegetation. It is necessary to identify and maintain key areas to protect the environment, biodiversity and important natural resources, while opening up other areas for agricultural production and other economic activities.

(f) Agriculture will for some time remain the most important economic sector in the country, on both the macro and micro scales. Agricultural development must increasingly take into account the negative impacts that it generates and seek ways and means of reducing them. Appropriate technology will have to be made available to farmers. For example, in some areas they will have to move away from extensive agricultural practices to more intensive 'environmentally friendly' ones. Thus, for different agro-ecological areas appropriate practices will have to be implemented.

(g) Haphazard mining practices, on both large and small scales, have to be checked. Checks and balances should be built into existing mining legislation, which is preoccupied with the issue of mining rights. Linked to this is the need to restructure economic liberalization policies to reflect the need to protect the environment in the course of extracting and processing natural resources. In this case, there is an urgent need to carry out assessments of the environmental impact prior to mining and environmental auditing of existing operations.

(h) The use and abuse of water resources will remain a contentious issue, especially as the population grows and the infrastructure for supplying water for its various needs (agricultural, industrial, domestic etc.) continues to fall behind demand. The preservation of catchment areas and a more effective utilization of existing sources are urgent requirements. Aspects such as the treatment and recycling of water will have to be considered, especially in urban and industrial environments.

(i) The plethora of urban environmental problems that exist today all over the country, coupled with the increasing rate of urbanization, clearly indicates that the current process is neither economically nor environmentally sustainable. The situation will remain so, unless sustainable policies are enacted and implemented. Towns and urban residents should not be viewed as financial liabilities. Instead, their dormant potential should be tapped and turned into national assets. There is an urgent need, in the light of the immense resource constraints and potential environmental disasters, for the people to be empowered and to participate in the management of their towns and cities.

(j) Given the growing nature of regional conflicts, and especially along the borders of Tanzania, refugees will continue to be a long-term problem entailing serious environmental impacts. In this case, a political solution may be the key to solving the problems. Conflict resolution mechanisms need to be put into place and implemented at a regional level with assistance from the international community. Short of that, the environmental repercussions will remain and grow, thus threatening a widening of regional conflicts.

Given the urgency of these matters, creating institutions and plans alone is far from adequate. What is also needed from the upper levels of government is a resolute political will and honesty to meet the challenges. At the lower levels the people need to be empowered to manage their resources sustainably, which implies that they must be stakeholders in the management of the environment. External support and cooperation need to come in simply to boost and accelerate the process. Only through this will there arise the possibility for improving and maintaining the quality of the environment while at the same time realizing sustainable economic and social development.

It is well known that government acts as well as most institutions established by acts pertaining to environmental pollution protection in general and air, water, sanitation and noise pollution in particular have weaknesses that render the acts and institutions ineffective to varying extents. Some of the key weaknesses are:

(a) the inadequacy of the acts in terms of coverage, content, depth detail and specificity as well as follow-up or enforcement mechanisms

(b) the lack of proper legal and technical framework at institutional level for complementary functioning in various aspects of environmental management

(c) the shortage of environmental experts who are conversant with land law and the corresponding shortage of lawyers and legal experts in the environmental field who would have served in handling cases as well as in developing legislation

(d) an inadequate arrangement on the part of institutions responsible for environmental management to promote public awareness about their roles, and about environmental laws and participation in facilitating their enforcement

(e) the inadequate legal and financial empowerment of the relevant institutions to withstand or resist political and other extra judicial interference on issues subject to environmental disputes

(f) the extremely low penalties for environmental pollution offences, and

(g) placing undue emphasis on (environmental) pollution effects rather than concentrating on preventive and precautionary as well as anticipatory measures.

To achieve this a number of priority policy instruments are suggested:

(a) approved land and other resources plans
(b) environmental impact assessments
(c) environmental legislation
(d) economic instruments, and
(e) environmental indicators and standards.

The complexity of environmental problems implies that a cross section of government agencies and sections of society must be involved in any action plan. The responsibilities cannot be left to the Ministry of Tourism, Natural Resources and Environment (MTNRE) alone and so there is a need for a clear definition of responsibilities. The MTNRE should play a coordinating role. The following are relevant in implementing the NEAP:

(a) the Planning Commission
(b) the Prime Minister's Office (Regional & Local Administration)
(c) the Ministry of Water, Energy and Minerals
(d) the Ministry of Lands, Housing and Urban Development
(e) the Ministry of Education and Culture
(f) the Ministry of Science, Technology and Higher Education
(g) the Universities
(h) the Ministry of Community Development, Women's Affairs and Children (MODWAC)

Legislation and enforcement of laws governing pollution
Tanzania has a considerable number of laws governing pollution control in the manufacturing sector but they arc poorly implemented and are often

fragmented (i.e., they are sectoral) in focus. There are several laws dealing with different kinds of pollution and several different authorities that are supposed to implement these laws. There is no institutional coordination in their enforcement, and there are deficiencies at the level of personnel and material means. They lack specifics and the fines are a mockery.

The national policy on science and technology
The national policy on science and technology (revised in 1993) emphasizes the maintenance of basic ecological factors for productivity and regeneration of natural resources. This implies recognition of the important links existing between sustainable development and sound environmental management practices. The policy thus emphasizes the preservation of biodiversity, cultural richness and the natural beauty of Tanzania.

Specific legal and institutional environmental measures
Several steps can be taken to improve the protection of the environment and to raise awareness of its importance. To do this it is necessary to:

(a) update the existing acts and institute new ones to ensure effective environmental pollution protection, to plug the existing loop holes and to keep the acts in line with changing technology and practices
(b) review all relevant legal provisions so that they are moulded to be preventive and precautionary as well as anticipatory, rather than curative and reactive as is the case now
(c) review penalties for environmental pollution offences to make them commensurate with the offences as well as to ensure their deterrent effect
(d) ensure that the laws are obligatory, and not provisional; firm and specific, not ambiguous nor conditional nor subject to opinion
(e) make all provisions in the acts on safeguarding of the environment legally obligatory and binding on agencies or persons responsible for causes of pollution
(f) provide for environmental aspects of land use changes in the acts, and monitor these to prevent pollution from unvetted activities following land changes
(g) harmonize the functions of institutions responsible for environmental issues to make their activities complementary, provide environmental management institutions with sufficient financial resources to ensure their smooth operation and hence more workable and effective environmental protection, and to empower these institutions in accordance with their obligations
(h) train both environmental experts, and lawyers and legal experts to

remove any weaknesses they may have in the area of environmental protection

(i) enlighten people on environmental matters including laws, and promote public awareness and participation in environmental protection issues, and

(j) promote transparency in handling environmental issues to prevent political or vested interests from interfering with verdicts of environmental experts on environmental disputes.

Relevant acts should include details of air and noise pollution (as well as other forms of pollution), to cover all sources. As such, non-conventional sources of pollution should also be covered including transportation facilities, entertainment and related activities and fires due to burning of solid wastes. This is only possible with the involvement of environmental experts who will identify the details needing coverage and law experts who will ensure proper formulation of legal provisions. Authorities that are charged with the duty of vetting investments in industries and other potential pollution causing projects should also, as a rule, incorporate environmental experts to vet environmental aspects of the project.

Human resources development and employment

Current status

The current high rates of unemployment stem from the economic crisis, which began in the late 1970s, and caused, inter alia, the contraction of the labour market. Some of the measures undertaken to deal with the crisis (e.g., Structural Adjustment Programmes) have also worsened, albeit for the short-term, the labour market situation. The formal sector (the public and private sector), which has been the major source of employment, is currently unable to offer employment opportunities for the majority of the 600,000 job seekers. Therefore, the relative importance of the public sector as a source of wage employment has declined substantially, while that of the private and informal sectors has grown. Out of the total population of 22.7 million people in Mainland Tanzania in 1990/91, labour force participation rate (the ratio of the economically active working age population) was 72.4 percent, 83.2 percent of which were in rural areas and only 16.8 percent were in the urban areas.

Formal sector employment
The formal sector is relatively small and offers employment opportunities of about 8.6 percent of total employment. The public sector (government and

parastatal sector) has been the largest employer of salaried workers, employing about 58 percent of total employment in the 1970s, and about 74 percent in 1984, before its contribution started declining since the early 1990s. Apart from economic crisis, the retrenchment exercise being undertaken by the government as part of the economic restructuring programme and the privatization of parastatal enterprises have contributed to a substantial reduction in employment levels.

Private sector (formal) employment
After being marginalized in the period following the Arusha Declaration, the private sector's role in the economy is now gaining prominence as a result of liberalization of the economy. This has resulted in the reduction of the dominating role of the public sector in productive and commercial enterprises in favour of the private sector, both local and foreign. Job creation within the private sector, however, remains small in numerical terms. According to World Bank figures, the number of people employed in the private sector has increased from 0.15 million in 1984 to 0.3 million in 1991.

Informal sector employment
The labour market is an important intermediating institution in the period of adjustment but here the record of job creation has been poor. Adjustment programmes have been associated more with retrenchment of workers from the public sector and from the declining import substituting industries. Informal sector activities grew in importance and became the most dynamic part of some economies as the formal sector activities have been going through some difficult phases in the course of adjustment. However, what is not certain is the extent to which the informal sector activities are dynamic and whether they are capable of transforming these economies.

The informal sector gained prominence as a source of employment after the economic crisis of the 1980s which exacerbated the problem of unemployment in the formal sector, and reduced, due to high inflation, real incomes and the purchasing power of the Tanzania shilling. This necessitated extra sources of income. For the majority of urban dwellers, for example, the informal sector is the only source of income (engaging nearly 60 percent of the urban labour force on either a full or part-time basis). However, for many low and middle level public employees and peasant farmers in rural areas it is a secondary source of income.

Agriculture
According to the Labour Force Survey (LFS), 92.7 percent of the employed population are engaged in the agricultural industry in the rural areas, and

37.9 percent in urban areas. This indicates the importance of agriculture in the economy and in employment creation. Currently, however, agriculture has been marginalized despite the fact that it is claimed to be the backbone of the economy. The rural to urban migration by youth is largely a result of the inability of agriculture to provide incomes equivalent to incomes earned in informal sector activities in urban areas. Seasonal and wage employment on plantations (especially in sisal, tea, tobacco and sugar estates) has become unattractive to youths.

The current human resources constraints facing developing economies are a good demonstration of the ineffectiveness and irrelevance of earlier policies and strategies in coping with emerging problems. The expansion of education and training institutions, the increase in enrolments and the rapid growth in numbers of high level educated manpower have not led to meaningful sustainable human resources development. The dominant approach with regard to the contribution of technical assistance in human resources development has been to fill gaps in high and middle level manpower requirements, and to help in the training and development of local capacities.

In post-secondary education and training, tertiary and technical training, Tanzania has too many (over 150) institutions, the bulk of which are owned by the government (74 percent) and parastatal corporations (14 percent). Total enrolment stands at an average of 12,000 students. Female enrolment is much lower than in earlier levels of education. In 1992 female enrolments were only 6 percent at Technical Colleges and 18.8 percent at the Universities. The other challenges facing higher education and training are high unit costs, high student/teacher ratios and unmotivated teachers, coupled with shortage of training equipment and other resources. Due to inadequate resources to run the institutions and sponsor students, the available capacity in tertiary training institutions is not fully utilized.

After independence mass mobilization activities aimed at boosting economic activity and eradicating poverty were developed. People were involved in self-help schemes and campaigns for improving the quality of life and health. Slogans such as "Mtu ni Afya, Chakula Bora, Kazi ni Uhai"[10] etc. were used to attract mass participation. Also, under the one party system of democracy people were involved in leadership and major decision making either directly or through representation.

The increasing incidence of rural to urban migration is a challenge to employment creation and social services provision in urban centres. As youths emigrate, the rural areas are increasingly being deprived of the young, educated and innovative population. The decline or destabilization in the human resources base in rural areas is mainly due to migration of youths to urban areas and to environmental degradation. The proportion of urbanized population more than trebled between 1967 and 1988 (from 5.7 percent to 17.9 percent). The United Nations (UN) estimates that by the year 2025 the urbanized population in Tanzania will reach 56.2 percent.

Serious under-utilization of the country's human resources exists. The Labour Force Survey identified incidence of low earnings, under-employment, and unemployment for the working population. In their 1988 report, the National Productivity Council discusses the falling trend in productivity in all sectors, and uses the low per capita GDP as an indicator of low productivity. The Human Resource Deployment Act of 1982 was a recognition of the problem of joblessness. Although it was not practicable to ensure growth in economic activity by applying legislation, adopting a policy on employment creation would have been more relevant than applying legislation and law enforcement organs of government.

Since the importance of the public sector as a significant absorber of labour is being reduced, the incoming private sector should be a major employer and trainer. However, the Tanzanian private sector of today is mainly composed of distribution industries that do not demand high levels of skill. Because the public sector is incapable of fully utilizing highly trained manpower, a brain drain has begun. Unsatisfactory working conditions, poor equipment and poor compensation packages contribute to this loss of trained personnel. Highly trained people, who are critically needed to man the economic recovery process, are leaving the country. Foreign experts recruited through various schemes, such as volunteer, technical assistance, project aid personnel schemes, do not foster the meaningful transfer of technology and sustainable capacity building. The challenge is that the availability of resources needed to improve the working conditions depends on manpower lacking in motivation.

In the longer term, the third phase government must develop a broad-based poverty alleviation programme with three major focuses:

(a) the rural focus specifically for arresting the decline of the human resources base and environmental degradation
(b) the gender focus, which is specifically geared towards women in development and women's empowerment, and
(c) a focus on other specific groups that are vulnerable and cannot benefit equally from general economic growth or social services provision.

In the industrial and minerals sectors, restructuring and diversification, taking into account domestic resource endowments, must receive priority. Science and technology development in this context is absolutely essential. Special emphasis must be placed on training cadres in the various aspects of design and the acquisition of relevant skills in order to operate and maintain the variety of installations thus established. The ultimate goal is self-reliance in basic operational and management skills in this sector.

Challenges and outstanding issues

The transition period is faced with great challenges as regards employment creation, including the needs to:

(a) revive the economy and stimulate a growth which stays ahead of population growth
(b) finalize and implement the National Employment Policy to address the problem of unemployment, and the need for coordination of efforts by various organizations
(c) target the groups most affected by the unemployment problem, among which are women, youth, the disabled and, in the short-term, the retrenchees, and
(d) eliminate constraints on employment generation in the informal sector.

Although the informal sector has a high potential for employment generation for the majority of school leavers and retrenchees, its expansion and development is currently limited. Factors which affect the sector's development include quality of products; management; marketing; accessibility to credit facilities, start up and working capital, and raw materials; unfavourable policy environment; and opportunities for training or retraining to improve informal sector operators' skills.

Economic and social policy options

In order to reduce significantly the problem of unemployment in the long-term, three areas need to be looked into.

Revival of the economy
All sectors with a potential for employment generation must be given attention by promulgating and implementing relevant policies to stimulate and enhance employment creation. Significant efforts need to be made in improving the agricultural sector in order to realize its potential for generating numerous employment opportunities (both wage labour and self employment) for smallholders, and to improve its productivity beyond subsistence level. Improvement of the sector (by increasing its cash generating capacity) and by facilitating the introduction of off-farm income generating activities would greatly contribute to the reduction in rural/urban migration by the youth. In addition, it is essential to improve and build new

social and economic infrastructures in the rural areas in order to increase agriculture's capacity to absorb extra labour.

As for the private sector, appropriate incentives and technical assistance are needed for adoption of new technology that leads to the speeding up of economic growth and hence employment generation. There is also a need to formalize or develop the informal sector and to allow it to benefit from these incentives and assistance.

Besides enacting an employment policy (which incorporates the informal sector), other areas that need attention include:

(a) increasing access to land
(b) development of infrastructure to cater for the sector
(c) accessibility to credit for informal sector operators (as the majority of operators do not qualify for credit from formal financial institutions)
(d) access to training and skill upgrading for increased productivity of informal sector operators
(e) improvement of the traditional apprenticeship system which is the major source of skills training for many informal sector operators, improvement of access to markets for inputs and products
(f) streamlining of procedures for informal sector operators to obtain licences, and
(g) coordination (in an institutional framework) of efforts that are being carried out by various government and non-government organizations (e.g., SIDO, NBC, International Labour Organization (ILO), DANIDA, Programme for Rural Integration and Development (PRIDE), German Bilateral Aid Agency (GTZ), etc.) to assist informal sector operators.

Education and vocational training systems
Emphasis should be placed on education and vocational training systems that prepare youth for self-employment. In this regard, curricula ought to be established that include subjects such as small business management, labour market information, project appraisal and book-keeping which can lead to self-employment. Thus, both academic education and vocational training should aim at training people to meet the demands of the labour market as opposed to training them for manpower requirements in the public sector, as has been the case since independence. In addition, vocational training should be flexible and responsive to the needs of the local community.

Promulgation of employment (including the informal sector) policy
This policy should create an environment conducive to employment promotion in all sectors (including the informal sector). It should define responsibilities among the various actors, and set up an institutional

framework to coordinate policy implementation and advise the government on effective employment promotion measures.

Women in development

Current status

According to the 1988 population census, women constitute about 51 percent of the population. Women also constitute about 75 percent of the population engaged in agriculture, which is the foundation of Tanzania's economy, accounting for over 40 percent of the GDP. Yet women's social and economic status remains low in spite of Tanzania's belief in the equality of all human beings, and in spite of the initiatives which have been taken to improve their situation. Tanzania is a signatory to the United Nations Declaration on Human Rights and has ratified the Convention on the Elimination of All Forms of Discrimination Against Women (CEDAW), which requires the government to, among other things, take legislative action and other special measures to implement the principle of non-discrimination against women in all spheres of life.

Tanzania, in its continued efforts to improve the social and economic status of women, has formulated a policy on women in development. The concept of women in development as used in the Tanzanian context is related to their integration in national development undertakings with the purpose of bringing about social, economic, ideological, and cultural liberation. Women are an important part of society and should participate fully in its development. However, their participation continues to face social, economic and cultural constraints, some of which are summarized in the following section.

Challenges and outstanding issues

Limited participation in decision-making at various levels
Women's participation in decision-making at all levels of society—social, economic, and political—is limited. Participation of women in non-agricultural productive and service sectors is generally low. Women constitute only about 20 percent of wage employment, with the majority clustered in low status positions. Women's representation in the political and civic spheres is also low. For example, in 1995 women comprised only 19 percent of the ministers in the union government. In 1990, only 11 percent of Members of Parliament were women, while in the judiciary women comprised only 7 percent and 16 percent of high court judges and resident magistrates respectively.[11]

Lack of access to resources
Customs and traditions in most societies in Tanzania still deny women the right to own land and to inherit wealth. Although Tanzania pursues a policy of equal rights for all, the denial of these rights to women is common because some customary laws and traditions that discriminate against women are recognized by statutory laws. Also, because they are poorly represented in income earning activities, most women have limited access to financial resources. Efforts by women to empower themselves by organizing into locally based groups for development activities are often constrained by an insufficient resource base.

Society's lack of appreciation of women's heavy workload
Women in their roles as producers, reproducers and carers continue to bear a heavy workload which negatively affects their health and, as they are primary care givers to children, the health status of their children as well.

Unequal access to education opportunities
Women have unequal access to education, particularly at higher levels. Representation of girls in primary education is about the same as that of boys. However, girls face disproportionate social and cultural constraints that affect their retention in school after enrolment. Opportunities for girls decrease as they climb the education ladder. For example, in 1994, females comprised about 43.9 percent of total secondary school enrolment.[12] At university level, in 1992/93 females constituted only 17 percent and 19 percent of the total enrolment at the University of Dar es Salaam and Sokoine University of Agriculture respectively.[13]

Absence of guidelines
The absence of guidelines on the development of women and strategies to equalize participation of women in all economic development activities also continues to limit women's participation.

Policy options

To equalize women's participation in development, it is necessary to:

a)   ensure that the policies governing the education and training system give girls and women equal access to education at all levels, especially in the science field where the problem of poor female representation remains pervasive

b)   put in place procedures to improve women's representation in management and high level decision making positions

c) speed up the process of reviewing and amending all laws which have provisions that discriminate against women, and
d) prohibit traditions which act as a barrier to girls' education, instigating procedures to ensure compliance.

Lack of information and communication is one of the obstacles to the improvement of women's social status. The government should facilitate massive information and communication campaigns. If women are more informed, they will be able to participate more in decisions that affect their lives. Awareness campaigns regarding women's heavy workload may also assist in lessening their workload. The Ministry of Community Development, Women's Affairs and Children has programmes whose purpose is to raise public and government awareness on gender issues. More support in terms of resources should be provided to this ministry to facilitate effective implementation from the national to the grassroots level.

Women's efforts to empower themselves through activities such as grassroots organizations and projects should be supported by the government in terms of policies that will provide an enabling environment for women to operate. For example, removing restrictions that make it difficult for women to get loans would facilitate women's access to credit.

Child survival, protection and development

Current status

Children are the future of the nation, and Tanzania recognizes the significance of taking care of these children to ensure their survival and development. It is with this recognition in mind that Tanzania has ratified the Convention on the Rights of the Child (CRC), the African Charter on the Rights and Welfare of the Child, and has prepared the National Programme of Action (NPA) for achieving the goals of CRC by the year 2000.

Assessment of the current status of children's health, nutrition, education, overall social wellbeing and safety show that a lot remains to be done if we are to ensure that our children grow up to become productive members of society. While achievements have been made in combating immunizable diseases, prevalence rates of other diseases such as malaria, diarrhoeal diseases and Acute Respiratory Infections (ARI) remain relatively high. Moderate malnutrition also remains an issue of concern.

Children in particularly difficult circumstances need special attention because of their situation. For example, orphans often lack adequate care to facilitate normal child development. The AIDS epidemic has caused a drastic increase in the number of orphans. Other kin members mostly take care of these orphans but care is often inadequate because of lack of resources. The country is also faced with a problem of an increasing number of children who live on the streets under harsh conditions. In 1994, about 3,500 children were living on the streets of Dar es Salaam. These children have often run away from domestic violence and child abuse in households.

Among older children, youth unemployment remains an issue of concern. The rate of unemployment among the youth is estimated to be 25 percent of the economically active youth population. Given the current estimate of economically active youths as six million, the percentage translates into 1.5 million unemployed youths.

The decline in enrolment rates in primary schools and the performance in examinations at form four and six levels discussed in Chapter 5 is worrying. Despite the small improvement in exam results in 1995, the low quality of education in schools is damaging to child survival and therefore must be addressed.

Policy implications

Children's health depends to a large extent on the effectiveness and efficiency of the health care system. As pointed out when describing problems facing the social sector, the health care system is constrained by under-funding in the health sector, and inequitable distribution of resources within the sector. The government should thus review the pattern of budget allocation in favour of child survival, and healthy physical and cognitive development as priorities.

Despite the government's continued efforts to decentralize responsibility for management and financing of primary education, efficiency and accountability in the management of primary education remain problematic. These problems have been identified as reasons for parents' and students' disillusionment with the education system. The government should put in place mechanisms for democratic accountability.

Implementation of policies and guidelines on children's enrolment and retention in schools should be strictly enforced. More effective disciplinary measures should be taken against parties who prevent children's enrolment and/or retention in schools. Because girls' and boys' enrolment in primary schools is almost at parity, the structure of public secondary school education should be readjusted to allow equal access to secondary education for both girls and boys.

Low teacher morale and under qualification are among the factors contributing to the declining quality in education. The government should motivate teachers by providing opportunities for self-advancement and by offering monetary and non-monetary incentives.

Although orphans are usually cared for by other members of the extended family, the government should issue clear guidelines on its role in assisting orphans who have no family members to care for them and those who have family members to care for them but receive inadequate care because of limited resources. There should also be clear guidelines and assistance to the youth who are willing to be self-employed but lack guidance and resources.

It is difficult to assess how children are treated in households. However, the government should find means of monitoring practices of child abuse in households and communities.

Civil service reforms

Current status

Since the advent of major structural reforms the economy has shown signs of recovery. However, the economic achievements of the recent years have not been matched by significant improvements in the institutional and administrative capacities of the government. Largely, this has been due to a lack of comprehensive and sustainable programmes to rehabilitate and enhance the capacities of public sector institutions, particularly those falling under civil service systems. This has justified the reforms and the strengthening of public sector management institutions to address the broad objectives of economic adjustment.

It is a generally accepted premise that Tanzania's civil service is bloated, inefficient and not effective in intervening to perform the state's traditional functions. This recognition led to the government's adoption of a Civil Service Reform Programme (CSRP) whose objectives were:

(a) to redefine the roles and functions of the government with a view to hiving-off those not considered a necessary part of its operations to an affordable scale, and restructuring its organization and operations to achieve efficiency and effectiveness in the delivery of public services

(b) to control the size and growth of government employment so that overstaffing is eliminated and the government can ultimately afford to competitively compensate its employees

(c) to improve the quality, capacity, productivity and performance of civil servants by strengthening systems and procedures for personnel recruitment, deployment, grading, promotions, training and discipline

(d) to rationalize and enhance civil service pay by eliminating the distortions and anomalies that have crept into the system, and by improving total compensation at all levels so that it meets minimum household living requirements, and

(e) to support the decentralization of government functions by rationalizing central and local government linkages, and facilitating further transfer of authority, responsibilities and resources to the districts.

The practice of civil service reform in Tanzania, which started in the late 1980s, was undertaken in two main phases. The first phase involved: determination of the optimal size of the civil service; developing a national training policy, with particular focus on civil service training; developing personnel control systems and workers' records coupled with automation and computerization to improve information systems and audit management; and strengthening of the civil service department and determination of appropriate administrative technologies and policies on procurement and maintenance, phasing-out and replenishment. The second phase (1993 to the present) has focused on the actual implementation of civil service reforms.

The ultimate objective of the CSRP is to attain efficiency and effectiveness in the delivery of public goods and services. To this end the key features of the CSRP include establishment of institutional mechanisms for technical leadership, supervision and coordination of the reform process, and adoption of multifaceted but coordinated, prioritized and sequenced interventions. The Programme is composed of the following six major components that constitute the main objectives and focus areas of the Civil Service Reform Programme:

a)   organization and efficiency reviews of government ministries
b)   pay reform through monetization of allowances and revised salary compression rates
c)   personnel management and control
d)   capacity building
e)   retrenchment and redeployment, and
f)   local government reorganization/reform.

By 1991 the bulk of the civil service was composed of primary school leavers (72 percent) and was over-manned by some 50,000 employees at all levels across government departments. The recommended retrenchment of 50,000 civil service employees has been achieved but the Structural Adjustment Credit (SAC) has not been accessed. After the retrenchment of 50,000 employees the total number of civil servants was about 330,000 of which 174,000 (52.7 percent) are local government personnel. About 85 percent of these local government staff, mainly employees in the education, health, roads and water services, are funded by central government grants. Primary school teachers alone constitute 100,000 employees.

Challenges and outstanding issues

In carrying out civil service reform, it has become evident that there has not been an integrated approach to addressing reform components. While Civil Service Reforms began with studies and experimentation in 1990 to 1992, it was not until 1992 that parastatals had a Commission to oversee their restructuring. As a result, if the recommendations of the Parastatal Sector Reform Commission (PSRC) are accepted, there is every likelihood of an increase in the size of the Civil Service resulting from a suggestion to the government that it reabsorb some of the earlier service "parastatals" such as training institutions. Similarly, some of the recommendations originating from the Civil Service Reform Programme are, if implemented, likely to increase the size and role of the parastatal sector, for example, from the recommended creation of agencies on the model of some European reforms. The challenge of coordination of civil service reforms is thus a very real one. Meanwhile, another task is to evolve a civil service that can be identified with professional competence and efficiency and which can bring about better service delivery.

The other problem concerns sustainability of reforms in the absence of foreign finance. The United Nations Development Programme (UNDP) supported the earlier measures and the new programme in place is now dominated by three agencies: the World Bank, the United Kingdom Overseas Development Organization (UK-ODA) and UNDP. This time funding (in soft loans and grants) extends to multimillions of dollars with little, if any direct government contribution. Like all donor-driven programmes the obvious question is that of sustainability of such reforms beyond donor support. With the critical bind of the government budget there is very little hope that internal resources will accommodate any medium-term pullout by donors.

How the government is set up is critical under the reform period. Tanzania's is a unitary government with a local government set-up. The earlier attempts at reforms, including the retrenchment before July 1993, concentrated on the central government even though local authorities generate the bulk of government employment (52 percent), while the central government generates the remaining 48 percent. Until now, no significant research or studies have been completed on the exact link (current and anticipated as the civil service is being trimmed) between the central government and these other sub-national levels of government. Reforms at central government level have a direct bearing on the performance and mandates of local government, and vice versa. Until a balance is struck on the kind and form of "fiscal and functional federalism" that is optimal for Tanzania, the reform exercise will not be too meaningful.

The overall structure governing the relationship between central government and local government must be revisited. The two acts, the Decentralization Act and the Local Government Act, exist together, and seemingly in conflict. As a result, the decentralization of authority to the local levels is negatively affected. This authority should reach the households. They must be involved in the management of the social facilities. Decentralization in all social sectors should be given priority, with greater powers devolving to regional, district and community levels.

The question of sequencing of actions, for example, compensation enhancement and retrenchment, demands attention. Some strategic action cannot be ruled out, especially for marginal cases. For instance, retrenchees who should be retiring or those who can be reabsorbed into the system should not at the same time benefit from retrenchment packages. Phasing out compensation and retrenchment is known to initiate some sensitive questions with regard to cost, sustainability and government credibility. From a cost perspective alone retrenchment should be completed before any significant compensation enhancement is effected. This in itself presupposes the presence of bold leadership at all senior government levels. Politics of patronage and the economy of affection made it difficult for the civil service to recruit the best and most competent employees. It is one thing to have a beautiful blueprint for civil service reform which advocates size reduction and skills improvement; but quite another to implement the desired reforms, because of entrenched vested interests.

An element that demands strength of resolve relates to reform of the military. The size of the army is larger than the requirements for maintaining the peace, securing our borders and so on. Support for liberation wars is no longer a preoccupation now. The Kagera War was fought seventeen years ago and yet significant demobilization has not yet been implemented.

The shrinkage of the public sector in absolute and relative terms is consistent with the changed role of the government.

Policy options

The government will continue the implementation of a programme of civil service reform covering six major elements: personnel control; "right-sizing" and redefining the civil service; pay reform; a comprehensive rationalization process on the basis of organizational reviews of each ministry; capacity building as ministries are rationalized; and local government reform.

Implementation activities for all ten ministries with completed Organization and Efficiency (O&E) reviews had been expected to begin early in 1996. O&E reviews for all the remaining ministries were to be completed by June 1996 with implementation following immediately after. To increase the transparency of civil service remuneration and broaden the income tax base, the government meant to design, by December 1995, and implement, by June 1996, a new salary structure in which in-kind benefits (with the possible exception of housing) will be monetized and all monetary allowances will be included in the basic wage.

The present size of the civil service is 330,000 of whom 39 percent work in central government; 8 percent in regional government; and 53 percent in local government.[14] The Civil Service Reform Programme seeks to reorganize ministries to fit a redefined role of government; reform staff pay based on performance; introduce new personnel management systems to provide better control and information; introduce training programmes to enhance work capacity; to retrench 50,000 civil servants; and to reform local government in order to strengthen its capacity and re-orient its functions. It is too early to make any firm assessment of this programme. So far some 47,000 have been removed form the payroll, including 14,600 "ghost workers". However, the wage bill has increased over the period of retrenchment due to high compensation rates.

The short-term policy action in the civil service reform requirement is that of identifying the needed resources. Since the components are integrated, any failure in any one of them is likely to spill over to the others, making the whole programme unworkable. The medium-term action, which requires mobilization of resources, must concentrate on a sequenced implementation of the programme in the order below:

(a) Organizational and efficiency reviews for both central and local government must be completed.
(b) Surplus workers must be identified and retrenched, and a "safety net" provided for them through redeployment opportunities, including the establishment of the Redeployment Fund.
(c) Foolproof controls on recruitment must be set up.
(d) There must be gradual pay enhancement as capacity building, including training, is instituted.

The last two items above will remain the permanent features of the civil service but the first two must be completed in (at most) three years to avoid reversals.

Other reform measures within the civil service that require immediate implementation include:

(a) reforming pay, with monetization of allowances and fringe benefits
(b) downsizing the army

(c) taking the necessary measures to hasten the effective creation (operationally) of the Tanzania Revenue Authority
(d) reforming and restructuring the government budget and instituting stringent expenditure control mechanisms, and
(e) a speedy computerization of all taxpayers.

lParastatal sector reform and privatization

Current status

Current policy reforms
One of the major objectives in the recent reforms has been to reduce the role of the state in production. The shortcomings of the public sector created under the Public Corporations Act 1992 have led the government to engage in an ambitious privatization programme. Several actions have been taken, including: divestiture through the creation of joint ventures; organizational changes promoting competition; and operational changes aimed at removing government controls and restructuring public enterprises. The role of the state in production has now been restricted to the provision of infrastructure and social services.

In many countries, public enterprise (PE) reform is a major component of policy strategies to accelerate economic growth. It consists of two distinct, but complementary approaches:

(a) divestiture, which involves privatizing public enterprises and encouraging private sector development, to enhance efficiency and shrink the relative size of the PE sector, and
(b) the corporatization approach, which involves enhancing managerial incentives and clarifying PE budget constraints so that PE performance improves without the government relinquishing ownership.

Divestiture objectives
A very important objective of divestiture is to encourage investment with a view to stimulating economic growth. Other objectives for privatization include encouragement of efficient allocation and utilization of resources, development of broader ownership, creation of jobs, and relief from financial burdens. This involves the sale of public enterprises and closure of those enterprises that are not viable. In undertaking this parastatal reform exercise, priority is given to optimal use of otherwise under-utilized assets, employment creation, profitability and acceptable financial and economic returns to the investors by way of profits and dividends, and government revenues. The policies for parastatal reform for a company's divestiture are

specific to that company and depend on its individual needs. The modalities for restructuring have been adopted by PSRC. These are:

(a) liquidation of those public enterprises that are considered to be non-viable
(b) divestiture of viable enterprises via the methods of joint-venture (trade sale), sale of shares, management buy-outs and buy-ins, and workers' buy-outs
(c) lease of public enterprises or assets, and
(d) performance contracts for those enterprises which continue to remain under public ownership.

Effects of divestiture programmes
371 parastatals were earmarked for either privatization or corporatization. 95 of these had been divested under the on-going PSRC exercise by the end of 1994. Of those divested, 34 were sold, either by share sale or sale of assets, 33 were placed under receivership or liquidated and 10 were closed. A further 15 were leased and the remaining 3 were subjected to a performance or management contract, or returned to former owners.

Positive results begin to emerge in terms of investment commitment and employment opportunities in specific sectors touched by this PSRC exercise. Substantial capital investment in modernization and rehabilitation is being made in all divested companies. One example is that of the former Morogoro Shoe Company (now privatized) where capacity utilization has increased from 4 percent to 37 percent and is expected to rise to 65 percent by the end of this year. Another case is Tanzania Breweries where six million cases of beer are expected to be produced this year at a profit, compared with 3.9 million cases produced at a loss two years ago. Other firms include Mwanza, Moshi and Morogoro Tanneries.

Outstanding structural problems

In the parastatal sector reform, efforts to limit borrowing have generally succeeded but there has been very little progress in restructuring the parastatals to increase productivity. The reform of parastatals has experienced some problems such as the inability to pay terminal benefits to deserving employees and at times failing to contribute to pension funds. By December 1994, the government had earned Tshs.4.4 billion and US$29.2 million from the privatization exercise. Some of this revenue is being utilized to pay terminal benefits and commercial debts that these parastatals had incurred.[15]

There is a feeling that the privatization of state-owned enterprises is the only viable "door" of entry into the modern industrial sector in the short to medium-term. These industries constitute the natural domain of private investors. The difficulties in assessing the value of assets, together with the overall poor economic situation (as well as political considerations) make these enterprises very unattractive candidates for privatization. The following specific problems need to be addressed:

(a) underdeveloped formal domestic capital markets, which make divestiture problematic
(b) industrial and technical institutional capacities, which are still subject to attempts to amend the Companies Ordinance and Investment Act with the intention of removing remaining obstacles to private sector participation (e.g., simplification of business licensing procedures) in the economy and enabling the country to benefit more adequately from such participation, and
(c) the need for the government to continue making efforts towards evolving a uniform and consistent land policy that would guide and regulate the allocation, ownership or leasehold, use, management and administration of land.

Possible solutions

The constraints to the direct sale of public enterprises seem to be insurmountable and this may therefore warrant alternative approaches to public enterprise reform. Reform and rehabilitation within the public sector may be one alternative to privatization but the difficulties in sustaining performance improvements can be considerable, especially after the crisis that instigated the reforms has dissipated. If the primary interest is in the promotion of market development, then reform may not be an effective alternative because it may not stimulate the private sector.

Reform of the parastatal sector is a key element of the government's Economic Reform Programme, the objective of which is to improve the operational efficiency of enterprises, to reduce fiscal and monetary pressure, and to promote wide participation by nationals in the ownership and management of business and economic activities. In order to encourage wide participation in the privatization programme, the government intends to develop a capital market, and has already drafted a bill for a Privatization Trust which would act as a vehicle through which some shares of enterprises being privatized would be held for future sale to the general public.

Indirect approaches lying between PE reform and complete divestiture (e.g., contracting-out, franchising, leasing) are likely to have little to offer for market development. However, the use of these approaches should remain among the instruments to be considered, as they can be appropriate in particular cases.

Privatization should be considered in a wider context, with the objective of promoting an institutional framework that is conducive to private sector development in the country. In that perspective, a sustainable policy environment must be created. The government should continue to support private sector development through the establishment of macroeconomic stability, elimination of unnecessary administrative requirements, the setting up of an appropriate incentive framework and improvements to infrastructure. It should rationalize, modify and modernize the legislative framework in a way that will encourage private sector development (including the enactment of a new companies act), and streamline the approval procedures to reduce the number of steps necessary to start a business. This requires the following important ingredients:

(a) stable macro policies, chiefly a small fiscal deficit, low inflation and a realistic exchange policy (liberalization of the exchange and trade system has already facilitated expansion of private sector activity)
(b) a considerable and predictable set of microeconomic incentives that are widely expected to be sustained into the future
(c) predictable rules of the game, including a stable political system that is seen to be legitimate, and a transparent and enabling legal framework established under the rule of the law
(d) attempts to amend the Companies Ordinance and Investment Act, with the intention of removing remaining obstacles to private sector participation in the economy (e.g., simplification of business licensing procedures) and enabling the country to benefit more adequately from such participation, and
(e) continued efforts by the government to evolve a uniform and consistent land policy that would guide and regulate the allocation, ownership or leasehold, use, management and administration of land.

The role of the state: revisiting the balance between the state and markets

The pattern and direction of civil service reform and parastatal sector reform should be guided by further reflections on the role of the state that is deemed most appropriate for Tanzanian conditions. It is useful here to draw some lessons from the experience of economic reforms in Africa.

The poor performance of African economies from the 1970s has been partly attributed to the prominent role that the state was allowed to play in production and in regulating economic activity. An important component of economic reforms has therefore been to curtail this prominent role of the state in the economy. One feature of economic reforms is their attempts to reduce the role of the state in economic management while giving greater leeway to the market and private sector. However, in the course of implementing economic reforms it has come to light that issues of governance and public administration, a functioning legal and regulatory frame work, and efficient financial and audit financial systems are also necessary components of the reform programme.

The speed and extent of the process of divestiture of state enterprises has varied among countries but in general the process has encountered political and social difficulties. In addition, the response of the private sector in buying up the public enterprises has been slow. These experiences call for a fresh look at this problem. In particular the balance between public and private enterprise activities needs to be revisited.

The implementation of economic reforms has revealed that more could be achieved in respect of rate of economic growth (level and sustainability), domestic savings and investment rates, structural changes and transformation to make the economies more resilient and lay the foundations for long-term sustained growth. History and theory suggest that the market alone is not well suited to bringing about these achievements. State intervention is called for. However, because the type of state intervention that was adopted in the past had its share in the poor performance of the economy it is advisable that useful lessons be drawn from that experience. The most important lesson is that the quality of state intervention needs to be improved and new forms of state interventions are required so that the market can be managed in the direction dictated by Tanzania's development goals and objectives.

State intervention in investment should be confined to selective promotion of direct investment in key strategic sectors and to the design of policies that encourage greater response from the private sector. Learning from experiences of the past, the new role of the state should be to seek control and guide economic activities by working through the market or by governing the market rather than working against the market. This implies using market mechanisms to guide the economic activity of private agents in the direction of the charted development goals and objectives. Support and incentives to the private sector should be performance orientated in the direction of these goals and objectives.

Successful transformation of production structures will call for preparation of strategic plans and effective industrial policies and trade and credit policies to encourage the development of comparative advantage in selected sectors. The capacity of the government should be strengthened to provide the essential services needed in a functioning market economy.

Economic reforms have tackled problems of governance through various reform programmes such as financial reforms, civil service reform, programmes seeking to create an enabling environment for the private sector, reform of investment codes, tax reforms and reform of various regulatory frameworks. However, these programmes have been introduced on a piecemeal basis as part of a selected sector rather than as an attempt to tackle the problem of governance in an integrated and direct manner.

External resource inflow: towards greater effectiveness

Tanzania's socio-economic development policy was based on the principles of the 1967 Arusha Declaration which perceived aid in the context of non-alignment (non-interference in national interests), and as complementary to local resources (non-dependence) and the national ability to repay external loans.

Foreign aid to Tanzania increased substantially after 1986 with the adoption of bold economic reform policies. However, recently, foreign aid appears to be on the decline due to slippages in implementation of agreed benchmarks particularly in the fiscal areas, as well as claims of rampant corruption. The future of foreign assistance to Tanzania will depend very much on the conviction of the donor community that the new administration will address the weaknesses of the former administration. Currently, Tanzania's investment programme is highly dependent on foreign aid. About 80 percent of development expenditure is donor funded. In some cases, donor funding is 100 percent as if the project will perpetually depend on donor funds.

Because aid has not been effective in bringing about a sustainable balance both in the internal and external sector, the debt burden has increased. All key ratios (debt/GDP, debt/exports, debt/imports, debt service) have increased tremendously since the early 1980s. The foreign debt burden is clearly demonstrated in the 1995/96 budget. The foreign debt, which was due for repayment in 1995/96, was about 60 percent of the national debt and 50 percent of the recurrent budget.

Again, because of overdependency on donor support, the government has overcommitted itself in terms of providing local counterpart funding. As a result, failure by the government to fulfill such obligations is now a common complaint by donors.

In reality, however, resource flows into Tanzania may not increase significantly on account of at least four factors: the stiff competition from other developing countries and recently from Eastern Europe; the budgetary constraints facing many donor countries; the global shortage of savings; and the aid fatigue which some donors have shown in recent years. If external resource inflows cannot meet the minimum requirements for sustaining a sufficiently high rate of growth then consideration should be given to at least three options—making do with lower growth, increasing domestic savings, or increasing productivity of investments. If the first option is ruled out then policy action will need to be directed towards domestic resource mobilization and improving the quality of investments and productivity of capital. In this context, greater attention must be paid to the efficient utilization of whatever aid resources may be available. The question relating to aid effectiveness deserves high priority.

As stated earlier, Tanzania does not have an explicit aid policy strategy. Formulation of aid strategy is a prerequisite for making external aid effective. A national aid strategy would ensure a "homemade" aid programme through putting in place a national framework for accepting and utilizing foreign aid. Top priority should be given to complementarity of aid to local resources and local efforts. In order to enhance accountability of aid and its complementarity to local resources, there is need to minimize offshore procurement. Currently, there are no national guidelines on procurement. Donor projects procure almost anything from abroad, ranging from stationery to vehicles. In future, procurement of goods and services abroad should be limited to those items that are not competitively available nationally. For example, it is strange that donors' projects still import office stationery abroad while it is now readily available locally. When foreign aid is spent directly in the recipient country it has a bigger impact (the backward and forward multiplier effect). Even procuring foreign goods from local dealers is very different from direct importation. By minimizing offshore procurements we would expand local capacities and enhance the revenue base.

Having tried to formulate and implement the two earlier programmes (NESP 1981 to 1982 and SAP 1982 to 1985) without success and without adequate support from donors, Tanzania has tended to accept the influence of IMF/World Bank and the donors' positions in economic policy, especially since 1986. This tendency is sustained by the perception that disagreement with IMF/World Bank would lead to withdrawal of support not only by these international financial institutions (IFIs) but also by other donors. This perception has tended to influence the relations between Tanzania and the donors, with Tanzania shying away from ownership of its development programmes, and has undermined local ownership of the development agenda. In addition, accountability has been asymmetrical, with low demand for the recipient to be accountable to its own political constituency. In addition the donors have not been sufficiently held accountable to the recipient for the outcome of aid. These conditions have tended to limit aid effectiveness.

Following the agreement with the IMF in 1986, aid relations between Tanzania and the donor community improved and aid flows resumed thereafter. Since then, however, Tanzania's ownership of development policy has been dramatically reduced. Initiatives in macro-economic policy and management, as well as sectoral development, have, since the 1980s, been taken over by the World Bank and the IMF. Donors have initiated many policy studies and sectoral policy formulations. At the level of project aid the perceived decline in the administrative capacity of public institutions, the decline in domestic resources and the perceived rising incidence of corruption have led to the establishment of parallel donor control structures for administering their own projects.

Too much aid leads to dependency, which may distort some dimensions of the development process by reducing autonomy, ownership and resilience of national institutions or by devaluing indigenous capacities, technologies and cultures. In addition, aid dependency has meant that during the period of economic crisis and reforms the initiative in the policy dialogue and in the formulation of solutions to Tanzania's pressing economic problems has shifted very much into the hands of the donor. Often, the discussion on key policy issues is initiated by the donors who also commission and implement many studies, for example, the Economic Policy Framework Papers.

While Tanzania has received substantial aid flows in the past, the future prospects for more aid are not that bright. The most likely scenario is that of a decline in aid flows in the future. This suggests that the most realistic policy option is to plan for phasing out aid over time. Planning for reduction of aid dependence should take a top priority primarily for Tanzania with support from her partners in development. There are at least three policy implications of this scenario: emphasis on domestic resource mobilization; greater utilization of local natural and human resources; and greater attention to national capacity building, especially in economic management. Aid should be sought only to fill gaps identified in sectoral programmes and in the capacity for economic management.

Some programmes are operated with little consultation and coordination with related activities within government and sometimes within the same ministry or even department. It is recommended that as far as possible donor supported projects should be located within the respective departments in ministries or other relevant national institutions. If these institutions are deemed weak then a case for enhancing their capacities could be made instead of operating projects in parallel structures.

Strengthening local government, the regional and district administration, community-based organizations and NGOs will contribute to the actual involvement and participation of society at all levels. Greater effort should be made to extend capacity building initiatives to these levels. This could be done by preparing a separate programme and document for Grassroots Capacity Building (GCB) that would be different from the other capacity building projects in the ministries.

One major factor that reduces the effectiveness of capacity building projects in economic management is the unconducive working conditions, especially the unrealistically low level of wages and salaries. These conditions make it difficult for staff and institutions to give adequate attention to the longer-term demands of economic management. The existing capacities cannot be utilized fully under these conditions. Action on this front has been rather slow and less coordinated as a programme. In order to raise the level of effectiveness of capacity building in the programmes it will be necessary to pay special attention to the civil service reform components which deal with working conditions of civil servants, including remuneration, and integrate the civil service into the whole programme of capacity building in economic management. Greater attention to the implementation of civil service reform may be a more effective approach to capacity building in government and economic management by government.

In order to build the competitiveness of local firms in the production of goods and services, inter-firm cooperation arrangements with technologically more advanced firms in the donor countries should be encouraged. The nature of inter-firm cooperation arrangements should reflect the relative capabilities of the partnering firms. These arrangements should be designed on commercial principles and technological capability and competitiveness. Under these arrangements, business negotiations would determine the extent to which the interests of the various parties are met. In such cases, certain conditionalities relating to procurement from donor countries can play a positive role in the sustenance of business partnerships under certain conditions. If such tied procurement enhances resource mobilization from the donor country in the interest of both partner firms, or enhances the technological capability of the weaker partner it may well be in the business interest of both firms to cooperate. To improve the quality of coordination in economic management, channelling aid to priority areas within a national framework of objectives is more conducive to enhancing aid effectiveness.

Regional and international cooperation

The volume of trade to many countries in the world is substantially influenced by the nature of the regional cooperation and trade agreements. This suggests the need for serious reassessment of the viability of small scale import substitution and far more consideration for regional cooperation and regional trade, which enable economies of scale to be tapped and international competitiveness to be attained. The unfolding of open competition accelerated by trade liberalization initiatives has shown that even to sustain regional markets, competition with other regions of the world will have to be faced sooner or later. There is always a danger of losing regional markets to competitors from other regions. Thus specific local and regional markets can be lost to others if continuous efforts are not made to develop competitiveness in terms of quality and price. The challenge now is whether regional cooperation arrangements and regional integration can be designed to facilitate (through investments and joint technological activities) the process by which firms and other institutions in Tanzania and other member states in the region can build up technological capabilities.

Regional cooperation and regional integration will need to be given appropriate interpretations under the new conditions of economic and political liberalization. The approach should rely more on market incentives and automaticity than on administrative discretion for its incentives and preferences. One implication of this approach is that public intervention should focus on policy formulation and a role which creates a regional policy environment that will enable market-based integration to work. The business sector should also be made more accessible and more participative than has been the case in the past. In order to promote the role of the business sector in regional economic cooperation and regional trade it is important that business associations establish modalities of cooperation, create strategic alliances and exchange information.

Economic reforms have been designed and implemented in the context of national level considerations. Regional implications have so far not been explicitly considered. National policy-making mechanisms and processes need to be designed so as to take into account regional implications. In this regard, there is need to establish a consistent mechanism for discussing the implications of various regional issues to national level policies and vice versa at national level or across interested parties. Regional macro-economic policy coordination and programming will need to be adopted to minimize inter-state economic distortions and harmonize various national policies.

In a number of sectors, the ability to remove constraints and meet investment requirements (including access to new techology) necessary for raising the level of competitiveness may require a regional rather than a national solution. For every such sector it is recommended that efforts should be made to identify cases where a regional solution is superior to a national solution. Such regional solutions should be articulated and ways of integrating them into national policy-making should be identified.

Changes in the world market and technological conditions that have taken place in the world economy in the recent past, particularly in the last decade, pose new challenges to development of a competitive economy in Tanzania. Four main categories of changes are most relevant: changes in market conditions; changes in technology hardware and software; changes in organization of production; and changes in globalization and regionalism. These market and technological changes are likely to have considerable implications in the shift in direction of knowledge-intensity of production and requirements for the kinds of capabilities that must be developed to cope with the changing situation. First, greater effort will be needed to monitor these changes with a view to adapting to the new situation. This will often imply selective adoption of new technologies in production and marketing at the right time and in the right applications according to the dictates of quality, precision, speed and productivity requirements. Second, greater effort will be required to create a conducive environment for the creation and development of core capabilities within firms and in the institutions that interact with those firms so as to cope with the changing conditions in the regional and world economy.

7. Summary and recommendations

Economic management

During the early 1980s, Tanzania's economy entered a state of crisis. The origins of this crisis go back to the 1970s and can be related to both external and internal factors. The external factors were those associated with changes in the world economies, the break-up of the EAC and the Kagera War. While the importance of these factors is recognized, the influence of domestic policy on such factors is limited. The most important internal policy management problems that contributed to the crisis included: the inadequate use of economic policies and incentives; the failure to put into practice self-reliance as an approach to development; the dislocation and erosion of local level development institutions (e.g., cooperatives, local councils); and the failure to unleash the potentials of private sector initiatives. When the economic crisis deepened in the early 1980s, economic reforms were introduced presumably to deal with some of the internal policy management problems. Included in these economic reforms were fundamental changes in the approach to managing the economy. After about a decade of implementing these reforms many lessons have been learnt and new issues have unfolded. This report takes stock of the current status of these reform efforts, draws out the lessons we have learned from the experience of implementing reforms, identifies the outstanding issues, and proposes some policy options.

Since the adoption of the reforms in 1986, there has been an improvement in economic growth as well as some improvement in macro-economic stability. Nevertheless, the sustainability of the current achievements has been threatened, largely by institutional and structural constraints. The most challenging structural and institutional constraints are manifested in the persistent budgets deficits, persistent balance of payments deficit (with official exports meeting only one-third of the import bill), a growing debt burden, a low level of domestic savings, and skewed investments in favour of quick-yielding trade-related and/or speculative activities. In addition, inflationary pressures are continuing, the capacity to manage the economy is still limited, and the institutional and legal framework have yet to be fully modified and restructured to suit the requirements of a market economy and private sector development. Furthermore, the effectiveness of the growth performance on poverty alleviation has been put in question, and doubts are being raised as to whether the achieved growth performance will also be accompanied by an economic transformation.

A series of reforms have been implemented using varying timings and different speeds. However, the various components of economic reforms are being introduced piecemeal without being guided by effective or strategic long-term priorities. The absence of an effective institutional mechanism to coordinate the various components of economic reforms is a major weakness. This mechanism should be composed of a team of high level officials from key ministries, members of the enterprise sector, the academic community, and NGOs. The secretariat should be the government institution responsible for policy analysis and economic management.

A burning issue requiring immediate attention relates to management of the budget. Action will be required in respect of revenue collection and expenditure control.

On the revenue side, steps have already been taken to establish the Tanzania Revenue Authority as the central body for assessing and collecting revenue as well as administering and enforcing laws related to revenue collection. However, it will take at least six months for TRA to be operational. Yet action needs to be taken immediately to meet the expectations of the people of Tanzania and the donors. The following recommendations are made:

(a) A mechanism for raising the performance level of the existing staff should be put in place. Since the existing staff would prefer to be absorbed into the new TRA, evaluation of their chances of this should take into account their performance in the revenue collection campaigns.

(b) As the substantial uncollected revenue from import taxes, domestic taxes and arrears related to import support funds are a stigma and contribute a great deal to the image of irresponsibility on the part of the government, attending to the issue of these arrears would instill a sense of seriousness and credibility.

(c) The collection of revenue may be accompanied by concessions tied to voluntary compliance, and payments could also be staggered, as many potential taxpayers are unlikely to be able settle all the arrears at once.

(d) In the medium-term, improved revenue collection should come from modernization (e.g., through computerized records); improving voluntary compliance (e.g., by lowering tax rates to reasonable levels); tax education; improving records; and instituting (on a consistent basis) penalties for tax evasion.

(e) Spending of tax revenue must be perceived as being proper and respectable.

(f) The tax base should be broadened so that it covers sectors in which many people are engaged, without discouraging their economic activities (e.g., in agriculture, small businesses and informal sector activities).

(g) Property tax should also be explored and emphasized.

On the expenditure side, action should be taken to show a sense of seriousness in expenditure control.

(a) The first step may be the announcement of a restructured and smaller government to convey the message that high priority is given to a small sized government and to the control of government spending.
(b) Efforts should be made to improve the budgeting system (e.g., by expenditure forecasting, monitoring and observance of expenditure limits).
(c) Expenditure control should give recognition to priority activities (e.g., infrastructure and basic social services). Priority expenditures should be identified at the budgeting stage. Budget estimates from ministries should be discussed thoroughly with the Treasury to determine priority activities jointly. This would assist in ensuring the ministries' adherence to spending only in these priority areas.

Donor support

Donor support will be crucial during the transition period. Considering the mood and fatigue among several donors, a new approach may have to be adopted to improve the relationship between Tanzania and the donor community. The guiding principle should be to demonstrate to all interested parties that the programmes for which donor support is sought have been designed with a view to reduce future dependence on donor support. This message should get across to donors and Tanzanians alike. Focus should be on capacity building in a way that will enhance self-reliance and ensure sustainability.

Monetary sector

In the monetary sector action needs to be taken on the following issues.

(a) Inflation has remained too high. Emphasis should be given to price stability with the objective of lowering the inflation rate to about 10 percent in 12 months time.
(b) Auctioning of treasury bills has also contributed to raising interest rates and denying the productive sector the credit it deserves. If the main objective of auctioning treasury bills has been to discourage the government from overspending, then more direct and less disruptive ways of controlling government spending should be sought.
(c) Government borrowing from the banking system should be discouraged. Already a cash budget system has been introduced. It

needs to be strengthened to eliminate government borrowing from the banking system, or from the market.

Financial sector reforms should be continued. While there is no need for drastic action to be taken on this front in the short-term, efforts in the medium to long-term should be directed towards the facilitation and further broadening of the financial sector, developing regional and rural financial markets and encouraging community-based financial intermediaries (for the mobilization of savings and credit financing).

Agricultural sector

In agriculture, priority should be given to action in:

(a) creating a conducive environment for increasing productivity
(b) improving access channels so that the initiative and potentials of many actors in this sector can be realized, the most important aspect of this being is physical access, which can be achieved through the improvement of regional roads and feeder road networks (starting with the major crop producing areas), allowing the contribution of many other actors such as extension agents, transport operators, distributors of inputs, buyers of agricultural products, and non-agricultural activists (e.g., rural industrialists) to be felt, and facilitating the activities of credit providers
(c) continuing to support the promising programme already in place to improve agricultural research and the extension system, and
(d) liberalizing and improving the facilitation of agricultural marketing, giving priority to setting up an institutional and legal framework which will facilitate the activities of marketing agents and aim to encourage competition in the context of clearly abiding to the "rules of the game".

Mining sector

In mining, the mineral sector policy strategy hopes to implement a series of reforms in its institutional, legal and regulatory framework. The emphasis that has been placed on private sector development of this sector should continue.

An area that is raising resentment among small miners and the public is the apparent indiscriminate and uncontrolled foreign participation in this sector. Foreign participation should prove that it could provide assistance in two areas—technology and marketing—and should take into account the following issues.

(a) Foreign participation should facilitate the upgrading of the technologies used in production and processing, and help to enhance networks and capabilities related to marketing.
(b) The kind of marketing assistance needed is not only that of purchasing the minerals being mined by Tanzanians but also that of putting transparent marketing arrangements in place.
(c) The practice of foreigners (in some cases illegally) hanging around mines waiting to buy minerals from ignorant small-time miners who lack any knowledge of marketing networks should be discouraged unless transparent marketing arrangements are made.

The Central Bank of Tanzania need not engage in marketing. The marketing function is a business activity that should be done by the business community. Local business companies should be helped to carry out marketing activities and to develop marketing capabilities by collaborating (in transparent ways) with foreign companies which possess better capabilities and networks in the world's mineral/ gemstone markets.

For the small miners, priority should be given to the facilitation and adoption of upgraded mining technology, the rationalization of marketing arrangements and the enhancement of compliance with the payment of taxes.

Industrial sector

The industrial sector lacks a policy to guide its activities. The first task is to hasten the on-going work on industrial policy formulation. The Confederation of Tanzania Industries (CTI) has submitted its input concerning industrial policy to the Ministry of Industries and Trade and the latter is currently working on the formulation of an industrial policy. This task should be speeded up, and the policy should facilitate broad-based industrial growth while at the same time improving employment-generating efforts and trade performances and increasing domestic and external competitiveness. Economic efficiency and technological dynamism should be given high priority. Industrial policy should be tailored to support the development of an efficient production system for both local and export markets. Priority should be given to the development of networks and linkages among sectors, and to assisting institutions and infrastructural support facilities.

Transport and communications

In transport and communications promising programmes are in place. What is now needed is support for their implementation. These programmes are very dependent on foreign funding. Programmes that favour the taking over and progressive replacement of donor funding with domestic financing should be put into place.

Priority should be given to rural road networks so as to catalyze activities in the rural sector. An institutional mechanism for constructing and managing the maintenance of rural roads should be put in place. The role and capacity of local administration and community-based institutions should be addressed to ensure that it can cope with the requirements of construction and maintenance of rural roads. The optimum use of domestic resources and labour-based technologies should be sought.

Social sector

The emphasis of the social sector strategy on the decentralization of decision-making powers to local institutions and communities is a step in the right direction. The emphasis placed on cost-sharing should be balanced with an equal emphasis on shared responsibility in influencing the management of delivery of services. Cost effectiveness should be given priority. For example, community participation in many aspects of primary health care can be very cost effective.

Access to basic social services should continue to be enhanced. Local level participation in mechanisms to ensure accessibility to basic social services by the poor should be encouraged. Pilot projects have been established to test new approaches to financing and delivery of social services. Lessons from these pilot projects should be reviewed and form an important input into the decision of how to proceed at the national level.

Coordination between line ministries, the Prime Minister's Office and local government should be revisited for the purpose of redefining coordination in the context of the proposed social sector strategy.

Export sector

In the export sector, a draft called the Export Development Strategy and Action Plan (1995-2000) has been prepared. It rightly emphasizes issues related to foreign strategic alliances to facilitate exportation and puts forward proposals on policy, institutions, infrastructure and capacity building.

(a) The first task is to analyze the report and formulate implementation strategies.

(b) A major step should be taken to form an expert development committee or council and draw membership from the government (Ministry of

Industries and Trade, Treasury, the Planning Commission, the Ministry of Agriculture, and the PMO), and the business sector associations (Tanzania Exporters Association (TANEXA), Tanzania Chamber of Commerce, Industry and Agriculture (TCCIA), CTI), the Board of External Trade (BET) and other relevant actors.

(c) In order to give it the importance it deserves, an arrangement should be made for the President to meet the Export Development Council once every three months to review progress in the sector.

(d) One major task of the Export Development Council should be the formulation of strategies for evolving a more dynamic export structure and developing new potentials in the export sector. The Export Development Council will also ensure that policies, as well as the infrastructure and institutional and legal framework, evolve in favour of the export sector's development.

Science and technology

Science and technology should be the basis for raising productivity, meeting basic needs, and attaining international competitiveness. There is need to raise the profile of science and technology in society and inculcate a science and technology culture for development.

Private sector development

Private sector expansion and initiative is still facing many obstacles, which result in a high cost of doing business. Initiatives need to be taken to enhance transparency in the operations of governing institutions, to reduce bureaucracy and to improve the legal framework and supportive infrastructure.

The approach to the conduct of both public and private sector business in the economy is not sufficiently transparent nor consistent with efficient market operations. The control mentality is still entrenched in the public sector, while the private sector still has an attitude and culture of earning quick high profits from investments in a non-competitive environment. New attitudes and a new cultures must be cultivated both in the government and business sectors so that they are consistent with facilitation and promotion of business in a competitive market environment.

Regional and international cooperation

Recent development in global trends and regional integration pose a challenge as to how Tanzania should respond to changes and carve an appropriate position for itself in the global economy. Markets are becoming more competitive and the speed of technological advance is increasing. The policy implications of the changing technological conditions are likely to surface at two levels: a focus on monitoring new and emerging technologies with a view to making policy decisions relating to adopting and learning the new technologies at the right time; and a focus on internal conditions of technological characteristics and demand conditions. Greater effort will need to be put into building the capacity to monitor the major trends in the regional and world economies with a view to responding and adapting the new situation to tap opportunities and avert threats. The new regionalism points towards the need to change the approach to regional integration by paying greater attention to the principles of variable geometry, subsidiarity, international competitiveness, business sector participation and incorporation of regional dimensions in national policy making.

8. Conclusion

The second phase government (1985-1995) initiated substantial changes in the way the economy was to be organized, managed and driven. The economic recovery programme which was introduced in 1986 initiated a shift from an administratively controlled and public sector dominated economy to a more market-oriented and private sector dominated economy. The government structure has also been undergoing change in the political system, the growing freedom of the press and the changing role of various groups in society. After ten years of reforms under the second phase government this book has examined the status of the reforms in various sectors, identified the main challenges that were to face the third phase government and the policy options that this government should consider.

This book has shown that the reform process is not yet complete. There are still many challenges to be faced by the third phase government. Progress has been made towards macroeconomic stability but sustainable stability is still elusive given the high inflation, balance of payments deficit and budget overruns. The exchange rate regime is better controlled but has yet to be stabilized. Progress has been made on many fronts in the direction of market orientation but the requisite institutional framework for a market economy is still fragile. The financial sector reform has opened up the financial system to the private sector and to competition but its effectiveness in financing development and mobilizing savings leaves much room for improvement.

The role of the public sector has been redefined with a view to readjusting the presence of the government in production and commerce. The main challenge is that of building the capacity of the state for development management in a market economy. Public sector reform has been initiated but it is far from complete. In particular the challenge of civil service reform is still on the agenda. An equally great challenge is in redefining the relationship between central and local government.

The reform process is a continuing challenge which needs effective governance and institutional mechanisms to be put in place consistent with the requirements of private sector development and a market economy. In this respect, the third phase government has a formidable task ahead.

130   **Notes**

1   J. Doriye. "Structural Adjustment Programmes in Tanzania: Progress and Prospects." Paper presented at the Economic Research Bureau workshop on "Beyond Structural Adjustment Programmes in Tanzania." Dar es Salaam, 2-4 August 1995.
2   World Bank. *African Development Indicators 1994-95* (Washington D.C.: World Bank, 1995).
3   M3 is broadly defined as the sum of the currency in circulation and commercial banks' non-government deposits, including foreign currency deposits.
4   Bank of Tanzania. *Economic and Operations Reports* (various years). Cited in Doriye 1995.
5   See B. Ndulu and J. Semboja, "The Development of Manufacturing for Export in Tanzania: Experience, Policy and Prospects," in G. K. Helleiner, ed., *The Transition to Manufacturing for Export in the Developing World: Problems and possibilities* (forthcoming, 1994), and J. Semboja et al, "The Import Duty Tariff Study," a report prepared for the Presidential Commission of Enquiry into Public Revenus and Taxation, Dar es Salaam, October 1991.
6   Kiswahili for "minibuses".
7   URT. Ministry of Education and Culture. *Basic Education Statistics in Tanzania (BEST) 1988-1992* (Dar es Salaam: Ministry of Education and Culture, 1993) and *Basic Education Statistics in Tanzania (BEST) 1991-1995* (Dar es Salaam: Ministry of Education and Culture, 1996).
8   World Bank. *Tanzania Social Sector Review* (Washington D.C.: World Bank, 1995).
9   See A. S. Bhalla ed., *Small and Medium Size Enterprises: Technology Policies and Options* (Westport: Greenwood Press, 1991).
10 Kiswahili slogan meaning "Man is Health, Health Food, and Work is Life/Living".
11 URT. *Analysis of African Women and Men: The Case of Tanzania* (Dar es Salaam: Bureau of Statistics and MODWAC, 1995).
12 URT. *BEST.*(1993 and 1996).
13 URT. *Analysis of African Women and Men* (1995).
14 These figures exclude 50,000 people working in national institutions such as Muhimbili Medical Centre, the Universities, and Training Institutions.
15 Speech given by the then Minister of Finance, Hon. Lt. Col. Jakaya Kikwete (MP), when introducing the Estimates of Public Revenue and Expenditure for the 1995/96 Financial Year, to the National Assembly, Dar es Salaam, June 1995.

Bank of Tanzania. *Economic and Operations Report.* Dar es Salaam: BOT, June 1992.

Bank of Tanzania. *Economic and Operations Report.* Dar es Salaam: BOT, June 1994.

Bhalla, A. S. ed., *Small and Medium Size Enterprises: Technology Policies and Options.* Westport: Greenwood Press, 1991.

Doriye, J. "Structural Adjustment Programmes in Tanzania: Progress and Prospects." Paper presented at the Economic Research Bureau workshop on "Beyond Structural Adjustment Programmes in Tanzania." Dar es Salaam, 2-4 August 1995.

Economic Research Bureau, University of Dar es Salaam (ERB) and the Economic Research Foundation (ESRF). Highlights of the Discussions and Recommendations of the Workshop on Selected Cooperation Aspects for Technological Capacity Building in Developing Countries. Geneva, April 1995.

Economic Research Bureau and the Economic and Social Research Foundation. "A study of Danish Aid Effectiveness in Tanzania" (draft report). Dar es Salaam, September 1995.

Jairo, D. K. "Foreign Participation in Mineral Resources Development in Tanzania with Particular Reference to Canadian Companies." Paper presented at the Prospectors and Developers Association (PDA) Conference, Toronto, 1993.

Jairo, D. K. "Mineral Resource Financing in SADCC." Paper Presented at Gaborone, Botswana, 1992.

Jairo, D. K. "Regional Efforts in Mineral Resources Development in the SADCC," a dissertation submitted to the Department of Mining and Metallurgical Engineering, McGill University. Montreal, 1989.

Jambiya, G. L. K. and F. Sechambo. "Towards Integrating Environmental Issues with Economic and Social Concerns in Tanzania." ESRF Research Paper. 1995.

JICA. *Rehabilitation of Dar es Salaam Water Supply.* Dar es Salaam: JICA, 1991.

Kimei, C. S. "Financial Sector: Past, Present and Future Challenges." Paper to an International Conference on Development Challenges and Strategies for Tanzania. October 1993.

Meena. H. E. "Significance of Price on Demand and Management of Urban Water Supplies in Tanzania." Unpublished MA dissertation. 1994.

Mtatifikolo, F. "Reforms in Systems of Governance: The Case of Civil Service Reforms in Tanzania," in L. A Msambichaka, H. P. B Moshi., and F. Mtatifikolo, eds., *Development Challenges and Strategies for Tanzania: An Agenda for the 21st Century.* Dar es Salaam: Dar es Salaam University Press, 1994.

Mushi, R. and S. M. Wangwe. "Review of Comparative Compensation Policies in Tanzania." Report to the World Bank. 1991.

Mwinyimvua, H. H. "The Impact of Macro-economic Policies on the Level of Taxation in Developing Countries: The Case of Tanzania." A dissertation submitted in partial fulfillment of the requirements for the degree of Doctor of Philosophy in Economics at the University of Dar es Salaam, 1995.

Ndanshau, M. O. A. "Financial Integration and Development in Sub-Saharan Africa: Constraints in Filling the Gaps in the Case of Tanzania." Paper presented at a World Bank-ESRF-ODA sponsored workshop in Dar es Salaam, 7-8 September 1995.

Ndulu, B. and J. Semboja. "The Development of Manufacturing for Export in Tanzania: Experience, Policy and Prospects," in G. K. Helleiner, ed. *The Transition to Manufacturing for Export in the Developing World: Problems and Possibilities* (forthcoming). 1994.

Nyirabu, C. M. "The Role of the Bank of Tanzania in the Development of the Primary Sector," in *Economic and Operations Report*.Dar es Salaam: BOT, June 1986. 42-46.

OECD. *Managing Technological Change in Less-Advanced Developing Countries.* Paris: OECD, 1991.

Padmore, G. "Government Participation in Mining Projects: Fiscal, Financial and Regulatory Implications for Developing Countries" in *Natural Resources Forum.* (A United Nations Journal), volume 16, no. 2 (May 1992).

Patnaik, U. C. "Reforms in the Banking Sector and the Task Ahead" in *State Bank of India Monthly Review,* XXXIII, no. 11 (November 1994): 516-22.

Rugeiyamu, Y. L. H. "Dodoma Region Water Supply and Sanitation Position Paper." Presented at a Regional Water Engineers' Conference, Iringa, November 1993.

Rutayisire, L. W. "An Evaluation of Possible Measures for Increasing Financial Market Competition in Tanzania," in M. S. D. Bagachwa, A. V. Y. Mbelle and B. Van Arkadie, eds., *Market Reforms and Parastatal Restructuring in Tanzania.* Dar es Salaam: Economics Department & Economic Research Bureau, University of Dar es Salaam, 1992. 91-113.

Semboja, H. H. and S. M. Wangwe. "Agricultural Sector's Potential." Background paper for Tanzania 1995 Country Economic Memorandum (CEM): World Bank. Dar es Salaam, 1995.

Semboja, J. et al., "The Import Duty Tariff Study." A report prepared for the Presidential Commission of Enquiry into Public Revenus and Taxation. Dar es Salaam, October 1991.

Tanzania Exporters Association (TANEXA). *Export Development Strategy and Action Plan (1995-2000).* Dar es Salaam, 1995.

Tanzania Government. *Results of the 1988 Civil Service Census Conducted on 30 March 1988.* Dar es Salaam: Government Printer, 1991.

Tanzania Government. *Rolling Plan and Forward Budget for Tanzania for the Period 1993/94-1995/96.* Dar es Salaam: Government Printer, 1993.

UN Department of Economic and Social Development (UN-DESD). "Size and Cost of the Civil Service: Reform Programmes in Africa." Report of a Seminar held in Accra, Ghana, 7-11 October 1991. 1992.

UNCTAD. "Country Case Study Submitted by the United Republic of Tanzania" TD/B/WG.5/Misc. 19. Geneva, March 1994.

UNDP. *Development Cooperation Report.* 1993.

United Republic of Tanzania (URT). *Analysis of African Women and Men: The Case of Tanzania.* Dar es Salaam: Bureau of Statistics and MODWAC, 1995.

URT. *The Banking and Financial Institutions Act, No. 12, 1991.* Dar es Salaam:

URT, 5 August 1991.

URT. Budget Speech by the Minister of Finance, Lt. Col. Jakaya Kikwete (MP) introducing to the National Assembly the Estimates of Public Revenue and Expenditure for the Financial Year 1995/96. Dar es Salaam, June 1995.

URT. *Economic Survey.* Dar es Salaam: Planning Commission, 1977, 1978, 1984, 1989, 1993 and 1994 issues.

URT."Financial Sector Restructuring in Tanzania: The Report and Recommendations of the Presidential Commission of Inquiry into the Monetary and Banking System in Tanzania." Dar es Salaam: URT, 19 July 1990.

URT. *The National Science and Technology Policy for Tanzania.* Dar es Salaam: URT, 1995.

URT. *Report of the Finance and Revenue Collection Probe Committee of the Board of Directors.* Dar es Salaam: National Urban Water Authority, September 1988.

URT. *Parastatal Privatization and Reform: Master Plan August 1993.* Dar es Salaam: Parastatal Sector Reform Commission, 1993.

URT. *Parastatal Privatization and Reform: 1993 Review and 1994 & 1995 Action Plan.* Dar es Salaam: Parastatal Sector Reform Commission, 1994.

URT. *Parastatal Privatization and Reform: 1994 Review and Action Plan for 1995 and Beyond.* Dar es Salaam: Parastatal Sector Reform Commission, 1995.

URT. Public Corporation Act. Dar es Salaam: URT, 1992.

URT. *The Rolling Plan and Forward Budget for Tanzania, (RPFB), for the period 1994/95-1996/97.* Joint publication by the President's Office, Planning Commission and Ministry of Finance. Dar es Salaam, 1994.

URT. *Statistical Abstract for 1992.* Dar es Salaam: Bureau of Statistics, February 1994.

URT. Ministry of Agriculture Statistics Unit and Bureau of Statistics. *National Sample Census of Agriculture 1993/94.* Dar es Salaam: Ministry of Agriculture, 1994.

URT. Ministry of Education and Culture. *Basic Education Statistics in Tanzania (BEST) 1988-1992.* Dar es Salaam: Ministry of Education and Culture, 1993.

URT. Ministry of Education and Culture. *Basic Education Statistics in Tanzania (BEST) 1991-1995.* Dar es Salaam: Ministry of Education and Culture, 1996.

URT. Ministry of Finance. "Current Economic Situation." Prepared for Consultative Group Meeting. Dar es Salaam, 1995.

URT. Ministry of Foreign Affairs. *Evaluation of the Netherlands Development Programme with Tanzania, 1970-1992.* The Hague: Ministry of Foreign Affairs, 1994.

URT. Ministry of Foreign Affairs and Finland. *Evaluation of the Development Cooperation between URT and Finland.* Helsinki: FCDC, 1994.

URT. Ministry of Foreign Affairs and Sweden. *Evaluation of Swedish Development Cooperation with Tanzania.* Stockholm: SASDA, 1994.

URT. Ministry of Health. *Health Statistics Abstracts.* Dar es Salaam: Ministry of Health, 1995.

URT. Ministry of Labour and Youth Development. *National Employment Policy.* Dar es Salaam: Ministry of Labour and Youth Development, 1993.

URT. Ministry of Labour and Youth Development. *Tanzania (Mainland) Labour Force Survey 1990-91.* Dar es Salaam: Ministry of Labour and Youth Development, 1992.

URT. Ministry of Science, Technology and High Education. "The National Science and Technology Policy for Tanzania" (draft). Dar es Salaam, 1993.

URT. Ministry of Water Energy and Minerals. *Water Policy.* Dar es Salaam: Government Printers, 1990.

URT. Throndheim University. *Macro-Economic Impacts of Import Support to Tanzania.* Dar es Salaam: CED, 1993.

Villalobos, J. "Bolivia's Strategy for Restructuring the State's Mining Sector and Promoting Private Investment in Mining," in *Natural Resources Forum,* Volume 13, No.3, August 1989.

Walde, T.W. *Third World Mineral Investment Policies in the 1980s: From Restriction Back to Business.* New York, December 1986.

Wangwe, S. M. "Industrial Restructuring in Tanzania: Implications of Changing External and Internal Conditions." In M.S.D. Bagachwa and A.V.Y. Mbelle eds., *Economic Policy Under Multipartism in Tanzania.* Dar es Salaam: Dar es Salaam University Press, 1993.

Wangwe, S. M. "Fostering Technical Capacity-Building in the United Republic of Tanzania and Ethiopia," Paper prepared for UNCTAD. 1995.

World Bank. *Adjustment in Africa: Lessons from Country Case Studies,* Washington D.C.: World Bank, 1994.

World Bank. *Adjustment in Africa: Reforms, Results and the Road Ahead.* Washington D.C.: World Bank, 1994.

World Bank. *African Development Indicators 1994-95.* Washington D.C.: World Bank, 1995.

World Bank. *Human Resource Development Survey 1993-94.* Washington D.C.: World Bank, 1995.

World Bank. *Tanzania Economic Report: Towards Sustainable Development in the 1990s.* 2 volumes. Washington D.C.: World Bank, 1991.

World Bank. *Tanzania: Public Expenditure Review.* 3 volumes. Washington D.C.: World Bank, 1989.

World Bank. *Tanzania: Public Expenditure Review.* 2 volumes. Washington D.C.: World Bank, 1994.

World Bank. *Tanzania Social Sector Review,* Washington D.C.: World Bank, 1995.

World Bank. *World Development Report 1989.* Washington D.C.: World Bank, 1989.

World Bank. *World Development Report 1994.* Washington D.C.: World Bank, 1994.

Mr. Buberwa
Planning Commission
(Human Resource Development)

Dr. E. Bukuku
PMO's Office
P. O. Box 3021
Dar es Salaam.
(Civil Service Reform)

Mr. D. K. Jairo
Ministry of Water, Energy and
Mineral
Resources
P. O. Box 9153
Dar es Salaam.
(Mining)

Dr. C. M. Luoga
International Labour Organization
(Employment Generation)

Mr. P. M. Lyimo
Planning Commission
P. O. Box 9242
Dar es Salaam.
(Reducing Aid Dependency and
Increasing the Effectiveness of the
Utilization of Aid)

Prof. R.B. Mabele
University of Dar es Salaam
(The Agricultural Sector)

Mr. H. E. Meena
CEEST
(Urban and Industrial Water Supply)

Prof. C. Migiro
Faculty of Engineering
University of Dar es Salaam.
(Science and Technology)

Dr. H. Moshi
University of Dar es Salaam

(Parastatal Sector Reforms and
Privatization)

Dr. F. Mtatifikolo
University of Dar es Salaam
(Civil Service Reform)

Mr. E. K. Mugurusi
Vice President's Office
P. O. Box 9372
Dar es Salaam.
(Environment)

Prof. G. Munishi
University of Dar es Salaam
(The Role of The State)

Mr. S. Mutabuzi
TANEXA
Dar es Salaam.
(Private Sector Development and
Export Promotion)

Dr. M. Ndanshau
University of Dar es Salaam
(Financial Sector Reforms and
Liberalization)

Mr. W. Ngirwa
Ministry of Agriculture & Livestock
Development
(The Agricultural Sector)

Mr. P. Noni
Bank of Tanzania
P. O. Box 2939
Dar es Salaam.
(Monetary Policy and Market
Determination of Interest Rates)

Mr. W. Nyachia
Ministry of Finance
P. O. Box 9053
Dar es Salaam.
(Industrialization Policy)

Dr. N. Osoro
University of Dar es Salaam
(Improving Revenue Collection and
Control of Government Expenditure)

Mr. Patrick Rutabanzibwa
Ministry of Water, Energy & Mineral
Resources
P. O. Box 9153
Dar es Salaam.
(Power Generating and Distribution)

Mr. Credo Sinyangwe
Tanzania Tourist Board
P. O. Box 2485
Dar es Salaam.
(Tourism)

Mr. A. N. Temba
Director of Planning,
Ministry of Transport and Communications
P. O. Box 9144
Dar es Salaam.
(Transport, Roads, Ports and Air Transport)

Mr. J. Zayumba
Planning Commission
(Social Sector: Health, Education, Water
and Sanitation)